T0150944

# Birds *of* Missouri

## Field Guide

Stan Tekiela

Adventure Publications
Cambridge, Minnesota

Edited by Sandy Livoti and Dan Downing

Cover, book design and illustrations by Jonathan Norberg

Range maps produced by Anthony Hertzel

**Cover photo: Dickcissel by Stan Tekiela**
**All photos by Stan Tekiela** except pp. 196 (all), and 286 (juvenile) by **Rick and Nora Bowers**; p. 160 by **Kevin T. Karlson**; p. 122 by **Brian E Kushner/Shutterstock.com**; p. 310 (female) by **Maslowski Wildlife Productions**; p. 104 by **Nuchie/Shutterstock.com**; p. 232 (displaying) by **Hartmut Walter**; pp. 42 (juvenile), 146 (both juveniles), 242 (juvenile), and 244 (in-flight juvenile) by **Brian K. Wheeler**; and pp. 188 (female), 234 (main), and 302 (female) by **Jim Zipp**

10 9 8 7 6 5 4 3
**Birds of Missouri Field Guide**
First Edition 2001
Second Edition 2021
Copyright © 2001 and 2021 by Stan Tekiela
Published by Adventure Publications
An imprint of AdventureKEEN
310 Garfield Street South
Cambridge, Minnesota 55008
(800) 678-7006
www.adventurepublications.net
All rights reserved
Printed in China
ISBN 978-1-64755-085-1 (pbk.); ISBN 978-1-64755-086-8 (ebook)

# TABLE OF CONTENTS

# WHAT'S NEW?

It is hard to believe that it's been more than 20 years since the debut of *Birds of Missouri Field Guide*. This critically acclaimed field guide has helped countless people identify and enjoy the birds that we love. Now, in this expanded second edition, *Birds of Missouri Field Guide* has many new and exciting changes and a fresh look, while retaining the same familiar, easy-to-use format.

To help you identify even more birds in Missouri, I have added 9 new species and more than 150 new color photographs. All of the range maps have been meticulously reviewed, and many updates have been made to reflect the ever-changing movements of the birds.

Everyone's favorite section, "Stan's Notes," has been expanded to include even more natural history information. "Compare" sections have been updated to help ensure that you correctly identify your bird, and additional feeder information has been added to help with bird feeding. I hope you will enjoy this great new edition as you continue to learn about and appreciate our Missouri birds!

# WHY WATCH BIRDS IN MISSOURI?

Millions of people have discovered bird feeding. It's a simple and enjoyable way to bring the beauty of birds closer to your home. Watching birds at your feeder often leads to a lifetime pursuit of bird identification. The *Birds of Missouri Field Guide* is for those who want to identify common birds of Missouri.

There are over 1,100 species of birds found in North America. In Missouri alone there have been more than 400 different kinds of birds recorded through the years. These bird sightings were diligently recorded by hundreds of bird watchers and became part of the official state record. From these valuable records, I've chosen 124 of the most common birds of Missouri to include in this field guide.

Bird watching, often called birding, is one of the most popular activities in America. Its outstanding appeal in Missouri is due, in part, to an unusually rich and abundant birdlife. Why are there so many birds? One reason is open space. Missouri is more than 69,000 square miles (179,400 sq. km), making it the twenty-first-largest state. Despite its large size, only about 6.1 million people call Missouri home. On average, that's only 88 people per square mile (34 per sq. km). Most of these people are located in and around only four major cities.

Open space is not the only reason there is such an abundance of birds. It's also the diversity of habitat. The state can be broken into three distinct regions, each of which supports a different group of birds.

The Glaciated Plains (Central Lowlands) in the northern half of Missouri is an open region with rolling hills, many streams and wooded river valleys. Although original vegetation was tallgrass prairie, it is now mainly agricultural. Many open-country birds are here, such as Horned Larks and Eastern Bluebirds, the latter being the state bird of Missouri. The northern Glaciated

Plains can be subdivided into northwest and northeast microregions. Northwest Missouri is dryer and lacks the trees of the northeast. In this area birds such as the Dickcissel and Northern Cardinal are more common. The wooded regions of the northeast attract such species as the Red-headed Woodpecker and House Wren.

Southern Missouri, called the Ozark Uplands or the Ozarks, is the most rugged area. Missouri's highest point and large tracts of forest are found here. Its oak-hickory forests are home to many birds such as Great Crested Flycatchers and Summer Tanagers.

Missouri's southeast corner is the lowest, flattest and wettest part of the state. Known as the Mississippi Lowlands, this region has been altered more than any other area in Missouri. It consisted of thick lowland forest in pre-settlement times. Now it is open, well drained and a good place to see species such as the Killdeer and Common Yellowthroat.

With several major rivers in Missouri, water also plays a large part in the state's bird populations. The Missouri River forms the border at the northwest corner. It also creates a natural division between north and south Missouri, cutting across the state from west to east. The Mississippi River forms the entire eastern border. Damming of several other major rivers in Missouri has created many of the state's largest lakes or reservoirs, such as Lake of the Ozarks, Truman Lake and Stockton Lake. These aquatic areas have created a substantial habitat for waterbirds such as the Double-crested Cormorant and Great Blue Heron.

Not only does Missouri have varying habitats, it has variations in the weather. Since the state extends over 300 miles (483 km) from north to south, the weather ranges greatly. While Missouri is considered a warm and humid state, the northern

...is considerably colder than the southern part in the
... It's not uncommon for the northern portion to remain
...ow freezing for extended periods in winter. During summer
...e central and southern portions of Missouri are extremely
warm, with average high temperatures in the nineties during
July and August.

No matter where you are in Missouri, there are birds to watch
in every season. Whether witnessing a migration of songbirds
in fall or welcoming back hummingbirds in spring, there is variety and excitement in birding as each season turns to the next.

## OBSERVE WITH A STRATEGY;
## TIPS FOR IDENTIFYING BIRDS

Identifying birds isn't as difficult as you might think. By simply
following a few basic strategies, you can increase your chances
of successfully identifying most birds that you see. One of the
first and easiest things to do when you see a new bird is to
note **its color.** This field guide is organized by color, so simply
turn to the right color section to find it.

Next, note the **size of the bird.** A strategy to quickly estim...
size is to compare different birds. Pick a small, a mediur...
a large bird. Select an American Robin as the mediu...
Measured from bill tip to tail tip, a robin is 10 inche...
Now select two other birds, one smaller and one ...
choices are a House Sparrow, at about 6 inches...
an American Crow, around 18 inches (45 cm). ...
species you don't know, you can now quickly ...
larger than a sparrow but smaller than a rob...
in your field guide to identify your bird, ...
species that are roughly 6–10 inches (1...
to narrow your choices.

Next, note the **size, shape and color...**
thick or thin, pointed or blunt, ...

birds, such as Northern Cardinals, have bills that are th...
strong enough to crack even the toughest seeds. Birds th...
nectar, such as Ruby-throated Hummingbirds, need long, ...
bills to reach deep into flowers. Hawks and owls tear their pre...
with very sharp, curving bills. Sometimes, just noting the bill...
shape can help you decide whether the bird is a woodpecker,
finch, grosbeak, blackbird or bird of prey.

Next, take a look around and note the **habitat** in which you
see the bird. Is it wading in a saltwater marsh? Walking along
a riverbank or on the beach? Soaring in the sky? Is it perched
high in the trees or hopping along the forest floor? Because of
diet and habitat preferences, you'll often see robins hopping
on the ground but not usually eating seeds at a feeder. Or
you'll see a Rose-breasted Grosbeak sitting on a tree branch
but not climbing headfirst down the trunk, like a Red-breasted
Nuthatch would.

Noticing **what the bird is eating** will give you another clue to
help you identify the species. Feeding is a big part of any bird's
...e. Fully one-third of all bird activity revolves around searching
...food, catching prey and eating. While birds don't always
... all the rules of their diet, you can make some general
...tions. Northern Flickers, for instance, feed on ants and
...cts, so you wouldn't expect to see them visiting a seed
... birds, such as Barn and Cliff Swallows, eat flying
...end hours swooping and diving to catch a meal.

...an identify a bird by **the way it perches.** Body
...ou differentiate between an American Crow
...wk, for example. Crows lean forward over
...while hawks perch in a vertical position.
...xt time you see an unidentified large

flight are harder to identify, but noting the **wing** **[size] and shape** will help. Wing size is in direct proportion to [body] size, weight and type of flight. Wing shape determines [wh]ether the bird flies fast and with precision, or slowly and [l]ess precisely. Barn Swallows, for instance, have short, pointed wings that slice through the air, enabling swift, accurate flight. Turkey Vultures have long, broad wings for soaring on warm updrafts. House Finches have short, rounded wings, helping them to flit through thick tangles of branches.

Some bird species have a unique **pattern of flight** that can help in identification. American Goldfinches fly in a distinctive undulating pattern that makes it look like they're riding a roller coaster.

While it's not easy to make all of these observations in the short time you often have to watch a "mystery" bird, practicing these identification methods will greatly expand your birding skills. To further improve your skills, seek the guidance of a more experienced birder who can answer your questions on the spot

# BIRD BASICS

It's easier to identify birds and communicate about them [...] know the names of the different parts of a bird. For insta[...] it's more effective to use the word "crest" to indicate the set [...] extra-long feathers on top of a Northern Cardinal's head than to try to describe it.

The following illustration points out the basic parts of a bird. Because it is a composite of many birds, it shouldn't be con- fused with any actual bird.

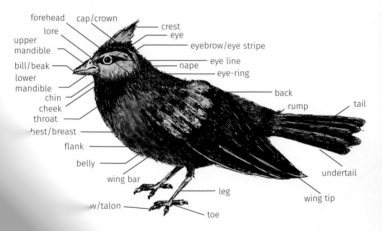

## [...]les

[...] a color palette like a bird's. Brilliant blues, [...]eds and iridescent greens are common [...]ral, male birds are more colorful than [...] This helps males attract a mate, [...]t me!" Color calls attention to a [...] the condition of his feathers, [...]y and potential for mating.

...ale birds that don't look like each other are called ...morphic, meaning "two forms." Dimorphic females ...e a nondescript dull color, as seen in Indigo Buntings. ...tones help females hide during the weeks of motionless ...bation and draw less attention to them when they're out ...eding or taking a break from the rigors of raising the young.

The males of some species, such as the Downy Woodpecker, Blue Jay and Bald Eagle, look nearly identical to the females. In woodpeckers, the sexes are differentiated by only a red mark, or sometimes a yellow mark. Depending on the species, the mark may be on top of the head, on the face or nape of neck, or just behind the bill.

During the first year, juvenile birds often look like their mothers. Since brightly colored feathers are used mainly for attracting a mate, young non-breeding males don't have a need for colorful plumage. It's not until the first spring molt (or several years later, depending on the species) that young males obtain their breeding colors.

Both breeding and winter plumages are the result of m... Molting is the process of dropping old, worn feath... replacing them with new ones. All birds molt, typ... a year, with the spring molt usually occurring in ... this time, most birds produce their brighter bre... which lasts throughout the summer.

Winter plumage is the result of the late... serves a couple of important functions... warmth in the coming winter seaso... it produces feathers that tend to... to camouflage the birds and... winter plumage of the male... is olive-brown, unlike its... summer. Luckily for us, ... Cardinal, retain their...

## Bird Nests

Bird nests are a true feat of engineering. Imagine co
a home that's strong enough to weather storms, large
to hold your entire family, insulated enough to shelter
from cold and heat, and waterproof enough to keep out r
Think about building it without blueprints or directions an
using mainly your feet. Birds do this!

Before building, birds must select an appropriate site. In some
species, such as the House Wren, the male picks out several
potential sites and assembles small twigs in each. The "extra"
nests, called dummy nests, discourage other birds from using
any nearby cavities for their nests. The male takes the female
around and shows her the choices. After choosing her favorite,
she finishes the construction.

In other species, such as the Baltimore Oriole, the female
selects the site and builds the nest, while the male offers an
ccasional suggestion. Each bird species has its own nest-
ding routine that is strictly followed.

can see in these illustrations, birds build a wide variety
es.

**cup
nest**    **pendulous
nest**    **cavity
nest**

natural items found in the
plant fibers (such as bark
ss, feathers, fur, or soft,

...from thistle. Some birds, including Ruby-throated ...birds, use spiderwebs to glue nest materials together.

...ortation of nesting material is limited to the amount a ...can hold or carry. Birds must make many trips afield to ...ther enough material to complete a nest. Most nests take four days or more, and hundreds, if not thousands, of trips to build.

A **ground nest** can be a mound of vegetation on the ground or in the water. It can also be just a simple, shallow depression scraped out in earth, stones or sand. Killdeer and Horned Larks scrape out ground nests without adding any nesting material.

The **platform nest** represents a much more complex type of construction. Typically built with twigs or sticks and branches, this nest forms a platform and has a depression in the center to nestle the eggs. Platform nests can be in trees; on balconies, cliffs, bridges, or man-made platforms; and even in flowerpots. They often provide space for the adventurous young and function as a landing platform for the parents.

Mourning Doves and herons don't anchor their platform n... to trees, so these can tumble from branches during high... and storms. Hawks, eagles, ospreys and other birds c... sturdier platform nests with large sticks and branch...

Other platform nests are constructed on the grou... grass and other vegetation from the area. Many... platform nests on the ground near or in wat... **form nest** moves with the water level, prev... and birds from being flooded.

Three-quarters of all songbirds cons... a modified platform nest. The sup... and attached firmly to a tree, shr... Next, the sides are constructe... leaves, which are woven tog...

added strength. The inner cup can be lined with dow[...] animal fur or hair, or soft plant materials and is conto[...]

The **pendulous nest** is an unusual nest that looks like a[...] hanging from a branch. Attached to the end of small branc[...] of trees, this unique nest is inaccessible to most predators an[...] often waves wildly in a breeze.

Woven tightly with plant fibers, the pendulous nest is strong and watertight and takes up to a week to build. A small opening at the top or on the side allows parents access to the grass-lined interior. More commonly used by tropical birds, this complex nest has also been mastered by orioles and kinglets. It must be one heck of a ride to be inside one of these nests during a windy spring thunderstorm!

The **cavity nest** is used by many species of birds, most notably woodpeckers and Eastern Bluebirds. A cavity nest is often excavated from a branch or tree trunk and offers shelter from storms, sun, cold and predators. A small entrance hole in a [tre]e can lead to a nest chamber that is up to a safe 10 inches [(25 c]m) deep.

[...] made by woodpeckers, cavity nests are usually used [...] by the builder. Nest cavities can be used for many [...] years by such inhabitants as Wood Ducks, mergan- [...] birds. Kingfishers, on the other hand, can dig a [...] et (1 m) long in a riverbank. The nest chamber [...] nnel is already well insulated, so it's usually

[...] of all nests is the **no nest,** or daycare [...] as Brown-headed Cowbirds, don't [...] d, the egg-laden female searches [...] d sneaks in to lay an egg while

wbird wastes no energy building a nest only to
ded by a predator. Laying her eggs in the nests of
rds transfers the responsibility of raising her young to
st. When she lays her eggs in several nests, the chances
ease that at least one of her babies will live to maturity.

## Who Builds the Nest?

Generally, the female bird constructs the nest. She gathers the materials and does the building, with an occasional visit from her mate to check on progress. In some species, both parents contribute equally to nest building. The male may forage for sticks, grass or mud, but it is the female that often fashions the nest. Only rarely does a male build a nest by himself.

## Fledging

Fledging is the time between hatching and flight, or leaving the nest. Some species of birds are **precocial,** meaning they leave the nest within hours of hatching, though it may be week before they can fly. This is common in waterfowl and shorebi

Baby birds that hatch naked and blind need to stay in th for a few weeks (these birds are **altricial**). Baby birds still in the nest are **nestlings.** Until birds start are called **fledglings.**

## Why Birds Migrate

Why do so many species of birds migrat is simple: food. Birds migrate to location as it is easier to breed where there is scarce. Rose-breasted Grosbea **plete migrators** that fly from the America to nest in the forests of newly hatched insects are

Other migrators, such as some birds of prey, mig[...] northern regions in spring. In these locations, they [...] voles and other small rodents that are beginning to br[...]

Complete migrators have a set time and pattern of migra[...] Every year at nearly the same time, they head to a specific wi[...] tering ground. Complete migrators may travel great distances, sometimes 15,000 miles (24,100 km) or more in one year.

Complete migration doesn't necessarily imply flying from the cold, frozen northland to a tropical destination. The Dark-eyed Junco, for example, is a complete migrator that flies from the far reaches of Canada to spend the winter right here in Missouri. This trip is still considered complete migration.

Complete migrators have many interesting aspects. In spring, males often leave a few weeks before the females, arriving early to scope out possibilities for nesting sites and food sources, and to begin to defend territories. The females arrive several weeks later. In many species, the females and their young leave [ear]lier in the fall, often up to four weeks before the adult males.

[...] species, such as the American Goldfinch, are **partial** [migrator]s. These birds usually wait until their food supplies [...] [be]fore flying south. Unlike complete migrators, partial [migrators mo]ve only far enough south, or sometimes east and [...] [ab]undant food. In some years it might be only a [...] [mile]s, while in other years it can be as much as [...] [kin]d of migration, dependent on weather and [...] [...]is sometimes called seasonal movement.

[...] [co]mplete migrators or partial migrators, [...] every third to fifth year or, in some [...] [the]se migrations are triggered when [...] [sca]rce. Red-breasted Nuthatches [...] their normal northern range [...] to overpopulation.

Many other birds don't migrate at all. Carolina Chickadees, for example, are **non-migrators** that remain in their habitat all year long and just move around as necessary to find food.

## How Do Birds Migrate?

One of the many secrets of migration is fat. While most people are fighting the ongoing battle of the bulge, birds intentionally gorge themselves to gain as much fat as possible without losing the ability to fly. Fat provides the greatest amount of energy per unit of weight. In the same way that your car needs gas, birds are propelled by fat and stall without it.

During long migratory flights, fat deposits are used up quickly, and birds need to stop to refuel. This is when backyard bird feeding stations and undeveloped, natural spaces around our towns and cities are especially important. Some birds require up to 2–3 days of constant feeding to build their fat reserves before continuing their seasonal trip.

Many birds, such as most eagles, hawks, ospreys, falcons and vultures, migrate during the day. Larger birds can hold more body fat, go longer without eating and take longer to migrate. These birds glide along on rising columns of warm air, called thermals, that hold them aloft while they slowly make their way north or south. They generally rest at night and hunt early in the morning before the sun has a chance to warm the lan and create good soaring conditions. Daytime migrators use combination of landforms, rivers, and the rising and sett sun to guide them in the right direction.

The majority of small birds, called **passerines,** migrate at Studies show that some use the stars to navigate. Oth the setting sun, and still others, such as pigeons, us magnetic field to guide them north or south.

While flying at night may not seem like a good idea, it's actually safer. First, there are fewer avian predators hunting for birds at night. Second, night travel allows time during the day to find food in unfamiliar surroundings. Third, wind patterns at night tend to be flat, or laminar. Flat winds don't have the turbulence of daytime winds and can help push the smaller birds along.

## HOW TO USE THIS GUIDE

To help you quickly and easily identify birds, this field guide is organized by color. Refer to the color key on the first page, note the color of the bird, and turn to that section. For example, the Red-headed Woodpecker is black and white with a red head. Because the bird is mostly black-and-white, it will be found in the black-and-white section.

Each color section is also arranged by size, generally with the smaller birds first. Sections may also incorporate the average size in a range, which in some cases reflects size differences between male and female birds. Flip through the pages in the color section to find the bird. If you already know the name of the bird, check the index for the page number.

In some species, the male and female are very different in color. In others, the breeding and winter plumage colors differ. These species will have an inset photograph with a page refer-ence and will be found in two color sections.

You will find a variety of information in the bird description sections. To learn more, turn to the sample on pp. 22–23.

cluded for each bird. Colored areas indicate frequently found. The colors represent the cies during a specific season, not the density, ds in the area. Green is used for summer, blue r year-round and yellow for migration.

fort has been made to depict accurate ranges, stantly in flux due to a variety of factors. Changing itat, species abundance and availability of vital ach as food and water, can affect the migration and of local populations, causing birds to be found in are atypical for the species. So please use the maps d—as general guides only.

female
p. 99

male

# Common Name

Range Map — *Scientific name* — Color Indicator

YEAR-ROUND
SUMMER
MIGRATION
WINTER

**Size:** measurement is from head to tip of tail; wingspan may be listed as well

**Male:** brief description of the male bird; may include breeding, winter or other plumages

**Female:** brief description of the female bird, which is sometimes different from the male

**Juvenile:** brief description of the juvenile bird, which often looks like the adult female

**Nest:** kind of nest the bird builds to raise its young; who builds it; number of broods per year

**Eggs:** number of eggs you might expect to see in a nest; color and marking

**Incubation:** average days the parents spend incubating the eggs; who does the incubation

**Fledging:** average days the young spend in the nest after hatching but before they leave the nest; who does the most "childcare" and feeding

**Migration:** type of migrator: complete (seasonal, consistent), partial (seasonal, destination varies), irruptive (unpredictable, depends on the food supply) or non-migrator

**Food:** what the bird eats most of the time (e.g., seeds, insects, fruit, nectar, small mammals, fish) and whether it typically comes to a bird feeder

**Compare:** notes about other birds that look similar and the pages on which they can be found; may include extra information to aid in identification

**Stan's Notes:** Interesting natural history information. This could be something to look or listen for or something to help positively identify the bird. Also includes remarkable features.

female
p. 127

male

# Eastern Towhee
*Pipilo erythrophthalmus*

**YEAR-ROUND**
**SUMMER**

**Size:** 7–8" (18–20 cm)

**Male:** Mostly black with rusty-brown sides and a white belly. Long, black tail with a white tip. Short, stout, pointed bill and rich, red eyes. White wing patches flash in flight.

**Female:** similar to male but brown instead of black

**Juvenile:** light brown, a heavily streaked head, chest and belly, long dark tail with white tip

**Nest:** cup; female builds; 2 broods per year

**Eggs:** 3–4; creamy white with brown markings

**Incubation:** 12–13 days; female incubates

**Fledging:** 10–12 days; male and female feed the young

**Migration:** complete to non-migrator, to southern states, South America; non-migrator in much of Missouri

**Food:** insects, seeds, fruit; visits ground feeders

**Compare:** American Robin (p. 231) is slightly larger. The Gray Catbird (p. 227) lacks a black "hood" and rusty sides. Common Grackle (p. 35) lacks a white belly and has a long thin bill. Male Rose-breasted Grosbeak (p. 49) has a rosy patch in center of chest.

**Stan's Notes:** Named for its distinctive "tow-hee" call (given by both sexes) but known mostly for its other characteristic call, which sounds like "drink-your-tea!" Will hop backward with both feet (bilateral scratching), raking up leaf litter to locate insects and seeds. The female broods, but male does the most feeding of young. In southern coastal states, some have red eyes; others have white eyes.

female
p. 131

male

# Brown-headed Cowbird
*Molothrus ater*

| | |
|---|---|
| **Size:** | 7½" (19 cm) |
| **Male:** | Glossy black with a chocolate-brown head. Dark eyes. Pointed, sharp gray bill. |
| **Female:** | dull brown with a pointed, sharp, gray bill |
| **Juvenile:** | similar to female but with dull-gray plumage and a streaked chest |
| **Nest:** | no nest; lays eggs in nests of other birds |
| **Eggs:** | 5–7; white with brown markings |
| **Incubation:** | 10–13 days; host bird incubates eggs |
| **Fledging:** | 10–11 days; host birds feed the young |
| **Migration:** | non-migrator in Missouri; moves around to find food in winter |
| **Food:** | insects, seeds; will come to seed feeders |
| **Compare:** | The male Red-winged Blackbird (p. 31) is slightly larger with red-and-yellow patch on upper wings. Common Grackle (p. ? has a long tail and lacks the brown European Starling (p. 29) has a sh |

**Stan's Notes:** Cowbirds are members of the blac approximately 750 species of parasitic birds wo only parasitic bird in Missouri. Brood parasi the nests of other birds, leaving the host bir Cowbirds are known to have laid their e 200 species of birds. While some birds incubate them and raise the young, e own. Look for warblers and other h their own size. Named "Cowbird" and cattle herds to feed on ins

winter

breeding

# European Starling

*Sturnus vulgaris*

**Size:** 7½" (19 cm)

**Male:** Glittering, iridescent purplish black in spring and summer; duller and speckled with white in fall and winter. Long, pointed, yellow bill in spring; gray in fall. Pointed wings. Short tail.

**Female:** same as male

**Juvenile:** similar to adults, with grayish-brown plumage and a streaked chest

**Nest:** cavity; male and female line cavity; 2 broods per year

**Eggs:** 4–6; bluish with brown markings

**Incubation:** 12–14 days; female and male incubate

**Fledging:** 18–20 days; female and male feed the you~

**Migration:** non-migrator to partial migrator; some ~ move to southern states

**Food:** insects, seeds, fruit; visits seed or s~

**Compare:** The Common Grackle (p. 35) h~ The male Brown-headed C~ brown head. Look for the ~ to help identify the Eu~

**Stan's Notes:** One of our most nume~ songs of up to 20 bird species a~ the human voice. Jaws are mo~ when closing, enabling the bird~ Often displaces woodpec~ nesting birds. Large famili~ a native bird; 100 star~ 1890–91 from Europ~

male

YEAR-ROUND

# Red-winged Blackbird
*Agelaius phoeniceus*

**Size:** 8½" (22 cm)

**Male:** Jet black with red-and-yellow patches (epaulets) on upper wings. Pointed black bill.

**Female:** heavily streaked brown with a pointed brown bill and white eyebrows

**Juvenile:** same as female

**Nest:** cup; female builds; 2–3 broods per year

**Eggs:** 3–4; bluish green with brown markings

**Incubation:** 10–12 days; female incubates

**Fledging:** 11–14 days; female and male feed the young

**Migration:** non-migrator to partial migrator

**Food:** seeds, insects; visits seed and suet feeders

**Compare:** The male Brown-headed Cowbird (p. 27) is smaller and glossier and has a brown head. The bold red-and-yellow epaulets distinguish the male Red-winged from other blackbirds.

**Stan's Notes:** One of the most widespread and numerous birds in the state. Found around marshes, wetlands, lakes and rivers. Flocks with as many as 10,000 birds have been reported. Males arrive before the females and sing to defend their territory. The male repeats his call from the top of a cattail while showing off his red-and-yellow shoulder patches. The female chooses a mate and often builds her nest over shallow water in a thick stand of cattails. The male can be aggressive when defending the nest. Red-winged Blackbirds feed mostly on seeds in spring and fall, and insects throughout the summer.

female
p. 149

male

SUMMER
MIGRATION

# Yellow-headed Blackbird

*Xanthocephalus xanthocephalus*

| | |
|---|---|
| **Size:** | 9–11" (23-28 cm) |
| **Male:** | Large black bird with a lemon-yellow head, breast and nape of neck. Black mask and gray bill. White wing patches. |
| **Female:** | similar to male but slightly smaller with a brown body and dull-yellow head and chest |
| **Juvenile:** | similar to female |
| **Nest:** | cup; female builds; 2 broods per year |
| **Eggs:** | 3–5; greenish white with brown markings |
| **Incubation:** | 11–13 days; female incubates |
| **Fledging:** | 9–12 days; female feeds the young |
| **Migration:** | complete, to southern states and Mexico |
| **Food:** | insects, seeds; will come to ground feeders |
| **Compare:** | The male Red-winged Blackbird (p. 31) is smaller and has red-and-yellow patches on its wings. Look for the bright-yellow head to identify the male Yellow-headed. |

**Stan's Notes:** Found around marshes, wetlands, and lakes. in deep water, unlike its cousin, the Red-winged Blackbird prefers shallow water. Usually heard before seen. Gives low, metallic-sounding call. The male is the only large with a bright-yellow head. He gives an impressive ma flying with his head drooped and feet and tail pointir steadily beating his wings. Young keep low and up to three weeks before they start to fly. Migrat of as many as 200 birds, often with Red-wing Brown-headed Cowbirds. Flocks of mainly m April; females return later. Most colonies cor

# Common Grackle
*Quiscalus quiscula*

YEAR-ROUND

**Size:** 11–13" (28–33 cm)

**Male:** Large, iridescent blackbird with bluish-black head and purplish-brown body. Long, black tail. Long, thin bill and bright-golden eyes.

**Female:** similar to male but smaller and duller

**Juvenile:** similar to female

**Nest:** cup; female builds; 2 broods per year

**Eggs:** 4–5; greenish white with brown markings

**Incubation:** 13–14 days; female incubates

**Fledging:** 16–20 days; female and male feed the young

**Migration:** non-migrator to partial in Missouri; will move around to find food

**Food:** fruit, seeds, insects; will come to seed and suet feeders

**Compare:** Male Great-tailed Grackle (p. 39) is larger and has a much longer tail. The European Starling (p. 29) is much smaller with a speckled appearance, and a yellow bill during breeding season. Male Red-winged Blackbird (p. 31) has red-and-yellow wing markings (epaulets).

**Stan's Notes:** Usually nests in small colonies of up to 75 pairs but travels with other blackbird species in large flocks. Known to feed in farm fields. The common name is derived from the Latin word *gracula*, meaning "jackdaw," another species of bird and a term that can refer to any bird in the *Quiscalus* genus. The male holds his tail in a deep V shape during flight. The flight pattern is usually level, as opposed to an undulating movement. Unlike most birds, it has larger muscles for opening its mouth than for closing it, enabling it to pry crevices apart to find hidden insects.

SUMMER
MIGRATION
WINTER

# American Coot
*Fulica americana*

**Size:** 13–16" (33–40 cm)

**Male:** Gray-to-black waterbird. Duck-like white bill with a dark band near the tip and a small red patch near the eyes. Small white patch near base of tail. Green legs and feet. Red eyes.

**Female:** same as male

**Juvenile:** much paler than adults, with a gray bill

**Nest:** floating platform; female and male construct; 1 brood per year

**Eggs:** 9–12; pinkish buff with brown markings

**Incubation:** 21–25 days; female and male incubate

**Fledging:** 49–52 days; female and male feed young

**Migration:** complete, to southern states, Mexico, Central America; winters in southern Missouri

**Food:** insects, aquatic plants

**Compare:** Smaller than most waterfowl, it is the only black, duck-like bird with a white bill.

**Stan's Notes:** Usually seen in large flocks on open water. Not a duck, as it has large lobed toes instead of webbed feet. An excellent diver and swimmer, bobbing its head as it swims. A favorite food of Bald Eagles. It is not often seen in flight, unless it's trying to escape from an eagle. To take off, it scrambles across the surface of the water, flapping its wings. Gives a unique series of creaks, groans and clicks. Anchors its floating platform nest to vegetation. Huge flocks with as many as 1,000 birds gather for migration. Migrates at night. The common name "Coot" comes from the Middle English word *coote*, which was used to describe various waterfowl. Also called Mud Hen.

female
p. 169

male

# Great-tailed Grackle
*Quiscalus mexicanus*

YEAR-ROUND

**Size:** 18" (45 cm), male
15" (38 cm), female

**Male:** Large, all-black bird with iridescent purple sheen on the head and back. Exceptionally long tail. Bright-yellow eyes.

**Female:** considerably smaller than the male, overall brown bird with gray-to-brown belly, light-brown-to-white eyes, eyebrows, throat and upper chest

**Juvenile:** similar to female

**Nest:** cup; female builds; 1–2 broods per year

**Eggs:** 3–5; greenish blue with brown markings

**Incubation:** 12–14 days; female incubates

**Fledging:** 21–23 days; female feeds young

**Migration:** non-migrator to partial in Missouri; will move around to find food

**Food:** insects, fruit, seeds; comes to seed feeders

**Compare:** Common Grackle (p. 35) is smaller, with a much shorter tail. Male Brown-headed Cowbird (p. 27) lacks the long tail and has a brown head.

**Stan's Notes:** This is our largest grackle. It was once considered a subspecies of the Boat-tailed Grackle, which occurs along the East Coast and Florida. A colony nester. Males do not participate in nest building, incubation or raising young. Males rarely fight; females squabble over nest sites and materials. Several females mate with one male. The species is expanding northward, moving into northern states. Western populations tend to be larger than eastern. Song varies from population to population.

in flight

# American Crow
*Corvus brachyrhynchos*

YEAR-ROUND

| | |
|---|---|
| **Size:** | 18" (45 cm) |
| **Male:** | All-black bird with black bill, legs and feet. Can have a purple sheen in direct sunlight. |
| **Female:** | same as male |
| **Juvenile:** | same as adult |
| **Nest:** | platform; female builds; 1 brood per year |
| **Eggs:** | 4–6; bluish- to olive-green with brown marks |
| **Incubation:** | 18 days; female incubates |
| **Fledging:** | 28–35 days; female and male feed the young |
| **Migration:** | non-migrator to partial migrator; moves around in winter to find food |
| **Food:** | fruit, insects, mammals, fish, carrion; will come to seed and suet feeders |
| **Compare:** | A common and familiar bird that is hard to confuse with any other. Much smaller than Turkey Vulture (p. 43), which has a naked red head. |

**Stan's Notes:** One of the most recognizable birds in Missouri, found in most habitats. Imitates other birds and human voices. One of the smartest of all birds and very social, often entertaining itself by provoking chases with other birds. Eats roadkill but is rarely hit by vehicles. Can live as long as 20 years. Often reuses its nest every year if it's not taken over by a Great Horned Owl. Unmated birds, known as helpers, help to raise the young. Extended families roost together at night, dispersing daily to hunt. Cannot soar on thermals; flaps constantly and glides downward. Gathers in huge communal flocks of up to 10,000 birds in winter.

soaring

juvenile

drying

YEAR-ROUND
SUMMER

# Turkey Vulture
*Cathartes aura*

**Size:** 26–32" (66–80 cm); up to 6' wingspan

**Male:** Large and black with a naked red head and legs. In flight, wings are two-toned with a black leading edge and a gray trailing edge. Wing tips end in finger-like projections. Tail is long and squared. Ivory bill.

**Female:** same as male but slightly smaller

**Juvenile:** similar to adults, with a gray-to-blackish head and bill

**Nest:** no nest or minimal nest, on a cliff or in a cave, sometimes in a hollow tree; 1 brood per year

**Eggs:** 1–3; white with brown markings

**Incubation:** 38–41 days; female and male incubate

**Fledging:** 66–88 days; female and male feed the young

**Migration:** complete, southern states, Mexico, Central America, South America, non-migrator in southern half of Missouri

**Food:** carrion; parents regurgitate to feed the young

**Compare:** Bald Eagle (p. 69) is larger and lacks two-toned wings. Look for the obvious naked red head to identify the Turkey Vulture.

**Stan's Notes:** The naked head reduces the risk of feather fouling (picking up diseases) from contact with carcasses. It has a strong bill for tearing apart flesh. Unlike hawks and eagles, it has weak feet more suited for walking than grasping. One of the few birds with a developed sense of smell. Mostly mute, making only grunts and groans. Holds its wings in an upright V shape in flight. Teeters from wing tip to wing tip as it soars and hovers. Seen in trees with wings outstretched, sunning itself and drying after a rain.

in flight

juvenile

crests

drying

# Double-crested Cormorant

*Phalacrocorax auritus*

MIGRATION
WINTER

| | |
|---|---|
| **Size:** | 31–35" (79–89 cm); up to 4⅓' wingspan |
| **Male:** | Large black waterbird with unusual blue eyes and a long, snake-like neck. Large gray bill, with yellow at the base and a hooked tip. |
| **Female:** | same as male |
| **Juvenile:** | lighter brown with a grayish chest and neck |
| **Nest:** | platform; male and female construct; 1 brood per year |
| **Eggs:** | 3–4; bluish white without markings |
| **Incubation:** | 25–29 days; female and male incubate |
| **Fledging:** | 37–42 days; male and female feed the young |
| **Migration:** | complete, to southern states, Mexico, Central America; winters in southern Missouri |
| **Food:** | small fish, aquatic insects |
| **Compare:** | The Turkey Vulture (p. 43) is similar in size and also perches on branches with wings open to dry in sun, but it has a naked red head. Twice the size of American Coot (p. 37), which lacks the Cormorant's long neck and pointed bill. |

**Stan's Notes:** Flocks fly in a large V or a line. Swims underwater to catch fish, holding its wings at its sides. This bird's outer feathers soak up water, but its body feathers don't. To dry off, it strikes an upright pose with wings outstretched, facing the sun. Gives grunts, pops and groans. Named "Double-crested" for the crests on its head, which are not often seen. "Cormorant" is a contraction from *corvus marinus*, meaning "crow" or "raven," and "of the sea."

male

female

# Downy Woodpecker
*Dryobates pubescens*

YEAR-ROUND

| | |
|---|---|
| **Size:** | 6½" (15 cm) |
| **Male:** | Small woodpecker with a white belly and black-and-white spotted wings. Red mark on the back of the head and a white stripe down the back. Short, black bill. |
| **Female:** | same as male but lacks the red mark |
| **Juvenile:** | same as female, some with a red mark near the forehead |
| **Nest:** | cavity with a round entrance hole; male and female excavate; 1 brood per year |
| **Eggs:** | 3–5; white without markings |
| **Incubation:** | 11–12 days; female incubates during the day, male incubates at night |
| **Fledging:** | 20–25 days; male and female feed the young |
| **Migration:** | non-migrator |
| **Food:** | insects, seeds; visits seed and suet feeders |
| **Compare:** | The Hairy Woodpecker (p. 53) is larger. Look for the Downy's shorter, thinner bill. |

**Stan's Notes:** Abundant and widespread where trees are present. This is perhaps the most common woodpecker in the U.S. Stiff tail feathers help to brace it like a tripod as it clings to a tree. Like other woodpeckers, it has a long, barbed tongue to pull insects from tiny places. Mates drum on branches or hollow logs to announce territory, which is rarely larger than 5 acres (2 ha). Repeats a high-pitched "peek-peek" call. Nest cavity is wider at the bottom than at the top and is lined with fallen wood chips. Male performs most of the brooding. During winter, it will roost in a cavity. Doesn't breed in high elevations but often moves there in winter for food. Undulates in flight.

female
p. 125

male

# Rose-breasted Grosbeak

*Pheucticus ludovicianus*

**SUMMER MIGRATION**

**Size:** 7–8" (18–20 cm)

**Male:** Plump black-and-white bird with a large triangular, rose-colored patch on the breast. Wing linings are rose-red. Large ivory bill.

**Female:** heavily streaked with obvious white eyebrows and orange-to-yellow wing linings

**Juvenile:** similar to female

**Nest:** cup; female and male construct; 1–2 broods per year

**Eggs:** 3–5; blue-green with brown markings

**Incubation:** 13–14 days; female and male incubate

**Fledging:** 9–12 days; female and male feed the young

**Migration:** complete, to Mexico, Central America and South America

**Food:** insects, seeds, fruit; comes to seed feeders

**Compare:** Male is very distinctive, with no look-alikes. Look for the rose breast patch to identify.

**Stan's Notes:** Most common in hardwood forests in the northern half of Missouri. Late to arrive in spring, early to leave in fall. Males arrive first in small groups, females join them several days later. Several males will visit feeders at the same time in spring. When females arrive, males become territorial and reduce visits to feeders. Young grosbeaks visit feeders with the adults after fledging. Both sexes sing a rich, robin-like song with a chip note in the tune, but male is much louder and clearer than female. The rose breast patch varies in size and shape in each male. "Grosbeak" refers to its thick, strong bill, used to crush seeds.

male

female

# Yellow-bellied Sapsucker

*Sphyrapicus varius*

MIGRATION
WINTER

**Size:** 8–9" (20–23 cm)

**Male:** Checkered back with a red forehead, crown and chin. Yellow to tan on the chest and belly. White wing patches are seen flashing in flight.

**Female:** similar to male but with a white chin

**Juvenile:** similar to female, dull brown and lacks any red marking

**Nest:** cavity; female and male excavate, often in a live tree; 1 brood per year

**Eggs:** 5–6; white without markings

**Incubation:** 12–13 days; female incubates during the day, male incubates at night

**Fledging:** 25–29 days; female and male feed the young

**Migration:** complete migrator, to southern states, Mexico and Central America; many winter in Missouri

**Food:** insects, tree sap; comes to suet feeders

**Compare:** Similar to other woodpeckers, but the male is the only Missouri woodpecker with a red chin patch. Look for the red chin and crown to identify the male Sapsucker, and the white chin and red crown to identify the female.

**Stan's Notes:** Found in small woods, forests, and suburban and rural areas. Drills rows of holes in trees to bleed the sap. Oozing sap attracts bugs, which it also eats. Defends its sapping sites from other birds that try to drink from the taps. Does not suck sap; rather, it laps the sticky liquid with its long, bristly tongue. A quiet bird, it makes few vocalizations but will meow like a cat. Drums on hollow branches, but unlike other woodpeckers, its rhythm is irregular. Makes short, undulating flights with rapid wingbeats.

male

female

# Hairy Woodpecker
*Dryobates villosus*

YEAR-ROUND

**Size:** 9" (23 cm)

**Male:** Black-and-white woodpecker with a white belly. Black wings with rows of white spots. White stripe down the back. Long, black bill. Red mark on the back of the head.

**Female:** same as male but lacks the red mark

**Juvenile:** grayer version of the female

**Nest:** cavity with an oval entrance hole; female and male excavate; 1 brood per year

**Eggs:** 3–6; white without markings

**Incubation:** 11–15 days; female incubates during the day, male incubates at night

**Fledging:** 28–30 days; male and female feed the young

**Migration:** non-migrator

**Food:** insects, nuts, seeds; comes to seed and suet feeders

**Compare:** Downy Woodpecker (p. 47) is much smaller and has a much shorter bill. Look for Hairy Woodpecker's long bill.

**Stan's Notes:** A common bird in wooded backyards. Announces its arrival with a sharp chirp before landing on feeders. Responsible for eating many destructive forest insects. Uses its barbed tongue to extract insects from trees. Tiny, bristle-like feathers at the base of the bill protect the nostrils from wood dust. Drums on hollow logs, branches or stovepipes in spring to announce territory. Prefers to excavate nest cavities in live trees. Excavates a larger, more oval-shaped entrance than the round entrance hole of the Downy Woodpecker. Makes short flights from tree to tree.

juvenile

YEAR-ROUND

# Red-headed Woodpecker
*Melanerpes erythrocephalus*

**Size:** 9" (22.5 cm)

**Male:** All-red head with a solid black back. White chest, belly and rump. Black wings with large white wing patches seen flashing in flight. Black tail. Gray legs and bill.

**Female:** same as male

**Juvenile:** gray brown with white chest, lacks any red

**Nest:** cavity; male builds with help from female; 1 brood per year

**Eggs:** 4–5; white without markings

**Incubation:** 12–13 days; female and male incubate

**Fledging:** 27–30 days; female and male feed the young

**Migration:** partial migrator to non-migrator; will move to areas with an abundant supply of nuts

**Food:** insects, nuts, fruit; visits suet and seed feeders

**Compare:** No other woodpecker in Missouri has an all-red head. The Pileated Woodpecker (p. 63) is the only other woodpecker with a solid black back, but it has a partial red head.

**Stan's Notes:** One of the few non-dimorphic woodpeckers, with males and females that look alike. Bill is strong enough to excavate a nest cavity only in soft, dead trees. Prefers open woodlands or woodland edges with many dead or rotting branches. Nests later than its close relative, the Red-bellied Woodpecker (p. 57), and will often take its cavity, if vacant. Unlike other woodpeckers, which use nest cavities just once briefly, it may use the same cavity for several years in a row. Often perches on top of dead snags. Stores acorns and other nuts. Gives a shrill, hoarse "churr" call.

male

female

# Red-bellied Woodpecker
*Melanerpes carolinus*

**Size:** 9–9½" (23–24 cm)

**Male:** Black-and-white "zebra-backed" woodpecker with a white rump. Red crown extends down the nape of the neck. Tan chest. Pale-red tinge on the belly, often hard to see.

**Female:** same as male but with a light-gray crown and a red nape

**Juvenile:** gray version of adults; lacks a red crown and red nape

**Nest:** cavity; female and male excavate; 1 brood per year

**Eggs:** 4–5; white without markings

**Incubation:** 12–14 days; female incubates during the day, male incubates at night

**Fledging:** 24–27 days; female and male feed the young

**Migration:** non-migrator; moves around to find food

**Food:** insects, nuts, fruit; visits suet and seed feeders

**Compare:** Northern Flicker (p. 159) has a black bib on its belly, not a reddish wash. The Red-headed Woodpecker (p. 55) has an all-red head.

**Stan's Notes:** Likes shady woodlands, forest edges and backyards. Digs holes in rotten wood to find spiders, centipedes and beetles. Hammers acorns and berries into crevices of trees for winter food. Returns to the same tree to excavate a new nest below that of the previous year. Undulating flight with rapid wingbeats. Gives a loud "querrr" call and a low "chug-chug-chug." Named for the pale red tinge on its belly. Often kicked out of nest hole by European Starlings. Expanding its range all over the country.

male

female

# Scissor-tailed Flycatcher
*Tyrannus forficatus*

SUMMER

**Size:** 10" (24 cm)

**Male:** White-to-gray head, neck, breast and back. Black wings with bright-pink wing linings, seen in flight. Faint-pink coloring on flanks and belly. An extremely long, black tail with patches of white.

**Female:** similar to male, with a much shorter tail

**Juvenile:** similar to adults, with a shorter tail, lacking pink underwings and sides

**Nest:** cup; female builds; 1 brood per year

**Eggs:** 3–5; white with brown-and-red markings

**Incubation:** 14–17 days; female incubates

**Fledging:** 14–16 days; female and male feed young

**Migration:** complete, to Central and South America

**Food:** insects

**Compare:** This flycatcher's extremely long tail and the distinctive black-and-white pattern with its pink wing linings make it hard to confuse with any other bird.

**Stan's Notes:** A wonderful summer resident. Like most flycatchers, it hunts for insects by waiting on a post or low tree and flying out to capture them as they pass by. Drops to the ground to hunt for insects much more than other flycatchers. Male performs an up-down and zigzag courtship flight, showing off his long tail. Sometimes will end the flight with a reverse somersault. When not breeding, often seen in large flocks. Roosts communally, with up to 200 individuals. Closely related to kingbirds.

female p. 175

male

# Lesser Scaup
*Aythya affinis*

WINTER

| | |
|---|---|
| **Size:** | 16–17" (40–43 cm) |
| **Male:** | Appears mostly black with bold white sides and a gray back. Chest and head look nearly black, but head appears purple with green highlights in direct sun. Bright-yellow eyes. |
| **Female:** | overall brown with a dull-white patch at the base of a light-gray bill; yellow eyes |
| **Juvenile:** | same as female |
| **Nest:** | ground; female builds; 1 brood per year |
| **Eggs:** | 8–14; olive-buff without markings |
| **Incubation:** | 22–28 days; female incubates |
| **Fledging:** | 45–50 days; female teaches the young to feed |
| **Migration:** | complete, to southern states, Mexico, Central America and northern South America; winters in Missouri |
| **Food:** | aquatic plants and insects |
| **Compare:** | Larger than American Coot (p. 37), which lacks male Scaup's white sides. Look for the distinctive white sides of the male Scaup to help identify. The male Blue-winged Teal (p. 173) is smaller and has a bright-white, crescent-shaped patch near base of bill. |

**Stan's Notes:** A common wintering duck in Missouri. Often seen in large flocks on lakes and ponds. Submerges completely to feed on the bottom (unlike dabbling ducks, which tip forward to reach the bottom). The male leaves the female when she starts incubating eggs. Egg quantity (clutch size) increases with the female's age. Has an interesting babysitting arrangement: groups of young (crèches) are tended by one to three adult females.

61

male

female

YEAR-ROUND

# Pileated Woodpecker
*Dryocopus pileatus*

**Size:** 19" (48 cm)

**Male:** Crow-size woodpecker with a black back and bright-red forehead, crest and mustache. Long, gray bill. White leading edge of wings flashes brightly during flight.

**Female:** same as male but with a black forehead; lacks a red mustache

**Juvenile:** similar to adults but duller and browner

**Nest:** cavity; male and female excavate; 1 brood per year

**Eggs:** 3–5; white without markings

**Incubation:** 15–18 days; female incubates during the day, male incubates at night

**Fledging:** 26–28 days; female and male feed the young

**Migration:** non-migrator

**Food:** insects; will come to suet and peanut feeders

**Compare:** The Red-headed Woodpecker (p. 55) is about half the size and has an all-red head. Look for the bright-red crest and exceptionally large size to identify the Pileated Woodpecker.

**Stan's Notes:** Our largest woodpecker. The common name comes from the Latin *pileatus*, which means "wearing a cap." A relatively shy bird that prefers large tracts of woodland. Drums on hollow branches, stovepipes and so forth to announce its territory. Excavates oval holes up to several feet long in tree trunks, looking for insects to eat. Large wood chips lie on the ground by excavated trees. Favorite food is carpenter ants. Feeds regurgitated insects to its young. Young emerge from the nest looking just like the adults.

soaring

# Osprey
*Pandion haliaetus*

**SUMMER MIGRATION**

**Size:** 21–24" (53–61 cm); up to 5½' wingspan

**Male:** Large eagle-like bird with a white chest, belly and head. Dark eye line. Nearly black back. Black "wrist" marks on the wings. Dark bill.

**Female:** same as male but slightly larger and with a necklace of brown streaks

**Juvenile:** similar to adults, with a light-tan breast

**Nest:** platform on a raised wooden platform, man-made tower or tall dead tree; female and male build; 1 brood per year

**Eggs:** 2–4; white with brown markings

**Incubation:** 32–42 days; female and male incubate

**Fledging:** 48–58 days; male and female feed the young

**Migration:** complete, to southern states, Mexico, Central America and South America

**Food:** fish

**Compare:** The juvenile Bald Eagle (p. 69) is brown with white speckles. The adult Bald Eagle has an all-white head and tail. Look for the white belly and dark eye line to identify the Osprey.

**Stan's Notes:** The only species in its family, and the only raptor that plunges into water feetfirst to catch fish. Always near water. Can hover for a few seconds before diving. Carries fish in a head-first position for better aerodynamics. Wings angle back in flight. Often harassed by Bald Eagles for its catch. Gives a high-pitched, whistle-like call, often calling in flight as a warning. Mates have a long-term pair bond. May not migrate to the same wintering grounds. Was nearly extinct but is now doing well.

in flight

juvenile

# Black-crowned Night-Heron
*Nycticorax nycticorax*

SUMMER

**Size:** 22–27" (56–69 cm); up to 3½' wingspan

**Male:** A stocky, hunched, and inactive heron with black back and crown, white belly and gray wings. Long, dark bill and bright-red eyes. Short, dull-yellow legs. Breeding adult has 2 long, white plumes on crown.

**Female:** same as male

**Juvenile:** golden-brown head and back with white spots, streaked breast, yellow-orange eyes, brown bill

**Nest:** platform; female and male build; 1 brood per year

**Eggs:** 3–5; light blue without markings

**Incubation:** 24–26 days; female and male incubate

**Fledging:** 42–48 days; female and male feed the young

**Migration:** complete, to southern states, Mexico and Central America

**Food:** fish, aquatic insects

**Compare:** A perching Great Blue Heron (p. 253) looks twice the size of a Black-crowned. Look for a short-necked heron with a black back and crown.

**Stan's Notes:** A very secretive bird, this heron is most active near dawn and dusk (crepuscular). It hunts alone, but it nests in small colonies. Roosts in trees during the day. Often squawks if disturbed from the daytime roost. Often seen being harassed by other herons during days. Stalks quiet backwaters in search of small fish and crabs.

soaring

juvenile

soaring
juvenile

# Bald Eagle
*Haliaeetus leucocephalus*

YEAR-ROUND

**Size:** 31–37" (79–94 cm); up to 7½' wingspan

**Male:** White head and tail contrast sharply with the dark-brown-to-black body and wings. Large, curved yellow bill and yellow feet.

**Female:** same as male but larger

**Juvenile:** dark brown with white speckles and spots on the body and wings; gray bill

**Nest:** massive platform, usually in a tree; female and male build; 1 brood per year

**Eggs:** 2–3; off-white without markings

**Incubation:** 34–36 days; female and male incubate

**Fledging:** 75–90 days; female and male feed the young

**Migration:** partial migrator, to southeastern states; winters along the Mississippi and Missouri rivers

**Food:** fish, carrion, birds (mainly ducks)

**Compare:** The Turkey Vulture (p. 43) lacks the white head and white tail of adult Bald Eagle. Turkey Vulture has two-toned wings and flies with its wings in a V shape, unlike the straight-out wing position of the Eagle.

**Stan's Notes:** Nearly became extinct due to DDT poisoning and illegal killing. Returns to the same nest each year, adding more sticks and enlarging it to huge proportions, at times up to 1,000 pounds (450 kg). In their midair mating ritual, one eagle flips upside down and locks talons with another. Both tumble, then break apart to continue flight. Not uncommon for juveniles to perform this mating ritual even though they have not reached breeding age. Long-term pair bond but will switch mates when not successful at reproducing. Juveniles attain the white head and tail at 4–5 years of age.

69

male

female
p. 99

SUMMER

# Indigo Bunting
*Passerina cyanea*

**Size:** 5½" (14 cm)

**Male:** Vibrant-blue finch-like bird. Dark markings scattered on wings and tail.

**Female:** light-brown with faint markings

**Juvenile:** similar to female

**Nest:** cup, female builds; 2 broods per year

**Eggs:** 3–4; pale blue without markings

**Incubation:** 12–13 days; female incubates

**Fledging:** 10–11 days; female feeds the young

**Migration:** complete, to Mexico, Central America and South America

**Food:** insects, seeds, fruit; will visit seed feeders

**Compare:** The male Blue Grosbeak (p. 73) is larger and has a large bill and chestnut-colored wing bars. The male Eastern Bluebird (p. 75) is larger and has a rusty-red breast.

**Stan's Notes:** Seen along woodland edges and in parks and yards, feeding on insects. Comes to seed feeders early in spring, before insects are plentiful. Usually only the males are noticed. The male often sings from treetops to attract a mate. The female is quiet. Actually a gray bird, without blue pigment in its feathers: like Blue Jays and other blue birds, sunlight is refracted within the structure of the feathers, making them appear blue. Plumage is iridescent in direct sun, duller in shade. Molts in spring to acquire body feathers with gray tips, which quickly wear off, revealing the bright-blue plumage. Molts in fall and appears like the female during winter. Migrates at night in flocks of 5–10 birds. Males return before the females and juveniles, often to the nest site of the preceding year. Juveniles move to within a mile of their birth site.

female
p. 123

male

SUMMER

# Blue Grosbeak
*Passerina caerulea*

**Size:** 7" (18 cm)

**Male:** Overall blue bird with 2 chestnut wing bars. Large gray-to-silver bill. Black around base of bill.

**Female:** overall brown with darker wings and tail, 2 tan wing bars, large gray-to-silver bill

**Juvenile:** similar to female

**Nest:** cup; female builds; 1–2 broods per year

**Eggs:** 3–6; pale blue without markings

**Incubation:** 11–12 days; female incubates

**Fledging:** 9–10 days; female and male feed the young

**Migration:** complete, to Mexico and Central America

**Food:** insects, seeds; will come to seed feeders

**Compare:** The more common male Indigo Bunting (p. 71) is very similar, but it is smaller and lacks wing bars. Look for two chestnut wing bars and a large heavy bill to distinguish it from the male Bunting.

**Stan's Notes:** Found throughout Missouri. A bird of semi-open habitats, such as overgrown fields, riversides, woodland edges and fencerows. Visits seed feeders, where it is often confused with male Indigo Buntings. Frequently seen twitching and spreading its tail. The first-year males show only some blue, obtaining the full complement of blue feathers in the second winter. It has expanded northward, and its overall populations have increased over the past 30–40 years.

# Eastern Bluebird
*Sialia sialis*

YEAR-ROUND

**Size:** 7" (18 cm)

**Male:** Sky-blue head, back and tail. Rust-red breast and white belly.

**Female:** grayer than male, with a faint rusty breast and faint blue wings and tail

**Juvenile:** similar to female but with spots on the breast and blue wing markings

**Nest:** cavity, vacant woodpecker cavity or nest box; female adds a soft lining; 2 broods per year

**Eggs:** 4–5; pale blue without markings

**Incubation:** 12–14 days; female incubates

**Fledging:** 15–18 days; male and female feed the young

**Migration:** partial migrator to non-migrator in Missouri

**Food:** insects, fruit; comes to shallow dishes with live or dead mealworms, and to suet feeders

**Compare:** Male Indigo Bunting (p. 71) is nearly all blue, lacking the rusty-red chest. Blue Jay (p. 81) is much larger and has a crest. Look for the rusty breast to help identify the Eastern Bluebird.

**Stan's Notes:** The state bird of Missouri and a year-round resident, bluebird populations occasionally drop due to unseasonably cold winters or cold, wet weather in spring. Although it is a permanent resident, many migrate each spring and autumn. Prefers open habitats, such as farm fields, pastures and roadsides, but also likes forest edges, parks and yards. Song is a distinctive "churlee chur chur-lee." A year-round resident that is joined by many northern migrants in winter. The rust-red breast is like that of the American Robin, its cousin.

**SUMMER**

# Barn Swallow
*Hirundo rustica*

**Size:** 7" (18 cm)

**Male:** Sleek swallow. Blue-black back, cinnamon belly and reddish-brown chin. White spots on a long, deeply forked tail.

**Female:** same as male but with a whitish belly

**Juvenile:** similar to adults, with a tan belly and chin, and shorter tail

**Nest:** cup; female and male build; 2 broods per year

**Eggs:** 4–5; white with brown markings

**Incubation:** 13–17 days; female incubates

**Fledging:** 18–23 days; female and male feed the young

**Migration:** complete, to South America

**Food:** insects (prefers beetles, wasps, flies)

**Compare:** The Cliff Swallow (p. 101) is smaller and lacks a distinctive, deeply forked tail. The Purple Martin (p. 79) is larger and has a dark-purple belly. The Chimney Swift (p. 85) has a narrow, pointed tail. Look for the deeply forked tail to identify the Barn Swallow.

**Stan's Notes:** Seen in wetlands, farms, suburban yards and parks. Of the six swallow species regularly found in Missouri, this is the only one with a deeply forked tail. Unlike other swallows, it rarely glides in flight. Usually flies low over land or water. Drinks as it flies, skimming water, or will sip water droplets on wet leaves. Bathes while flying through rain or sprinklers. Gives a twittering warble, followed by a mechanical sound. Builds a mud nest with up to 1,000 beak-loads of mud. Nests on barns and houses, under bridges and in other sheltered places. Often nests in colonies of 4–6 birds; sometimes nests alone.

male

female

# Purple Martin
*Progne subis*

SUMMER

**Size:** 8½" (22 cm)

**Male:** Iridescent with a purple-to-black head, back and belly. Black wings and a notched black tail.

**Female:** grayish-purple head and back, darker wings and tail, whitish belly

**Juvenile:** same as female

**Nest:** cavity; female and male line the cavity of the house; 1 brood per year

**Eggs:** 4–5; white without markings

**Incubation:** 15–18 days; female incubates

**Fledging:** 26–30 days; male and female feed the young

**Migration:** complete, to South America

**Food:** insects

**Compare:** Usually seen only in groups. The male Purple Martin is the only swallow with a very dark-purplish belly.

**Stan's Notes:** The largest swallow species in North America. Once nested in tree cavities; now nests almost exclusively in man-made, apartment-style houses. The most successful colonies often nest in multiunit nest boxes within 100 feet (30 m) of a human dwelling near a lake. Main diet consists of dragonflies, not mosquitoes, as once thought. Gives a continuous stream of chirps, creaks and rattles, along with a shout-like "churrr" and chortle. Often drinks in flight, skimming water, and bathes in flight, flying through rain. Returns to the same nest site each year; the males arrive before the females and yearlings. The young leave to form new colonies. Large colonies gather in fall before migrating to South America.

# Blue Jay
*Cyanocitta cristata*

**YEAR-ROUND**

**Size:** 12" (30 cm)

**Male:** Bright light-blue-and-white bird with a black necklace and gray belly. Large crest moves up and down at will. White face, wing bars and tip of tail. Black tail bands.

**Female:** same as male

**Juvenile:** same as adult but duller

**Nest:** cup; female and male construct; 1–2 broods per year

**Eggs:** 4–5; green to blue with brown markings

**Incubation:** 16–18 days; female incubates

**Fledging:** 17–21 days; female and male feed the young

**Migration:** non-migrator to partial migrator; will move around to find an abundant food source

**Food:** insects, fruit, carrion, seeds, nuts; visits seed feeders, ground feeders with corn or peanuts

**Compare:** The Belted Kingfisher (p. 83) has a larger, more ragged crest. The Eastern Bluebird (p. 75) is much smaller and has a rust-red breast. Look for the large crest to help identify the Blue Jay.

**Stan's Notes:** Highly intelligent, solving problems, gathering food and communicating more than other birds. Loud and noisy; mimics other birds. Known as the alarm of the forest, screaming at intruders. Imitates hawk calls around feeders to scare off other birds. One of the few birds to cache food; can remember where it hid thousands of nuts. Carries food in a pouch under its tongue (sublingually). Eats eggs and young from other nests. Feathers lack blue pigment; refracted sunlight causes the blue appearance.

# Belted Kingfisher
*Megaceryle alcyon*

YEAR-ROUND

**Size:** 12–14" (30–36 cm)

**Male:** Blue with white belly, blue-gray chest band, and black wing tips. Ragged crest moves up and down at will. Large head. Long, thick, black bill. White spot by eyes. Red-brown eyes.

**Female:** same as male but with rusty flanks and a rusty chest band below the blue-gray band

**Juvenile:** similar to female

**Nest:** cavity; female and male excavate in a bank of a river, lake or cliff; 1 brood per year

**Eggs:** 6–7; white without markings

**Incubation:** 23–24 days; female and male incubate

**Fledging:** 23–24 days; female and male feed the young

**Migration:** complete, to southern states, Mexico, Central and South America, winters in Missouri

**Food:** small fish

**Compare:** The Blue Jay (p. 81) is lighter blue and has a plain gray chest and belly. The Belted Kingfisher is rarely found away from water.

**Stan's Notes:** Usually found at the bank of a river, lake or large stream. Perches on a branch near water, dives in headfirst to catch a small fish, then returns to the branch to feed. Parents drop dead fish into the water to teach their young to dive. Can't pass bones through its digestive tract; regurgitates bone pellets after meals. Gives a loud call that sounds like a machine gun. Mates know each other by their calls. Digs a tunnel up to 4 feet (1 m) long to a nest chamber. Small white patches on dark wing tips flash during flight.

# Chimney Swift
*Chaetura pelagica*

SUMMER

**Size:** 5" (13 cm)

**Male:** Nondescript, cigar-shaped bird, usually seen in flight. Long, thin, brown body. Pointed tail and head. Long, backswept wings, longer than the body.

**Female:** same as male

**Juvenile:** same as adult

**Nest:** half cup; female and male build; 1 brood per year

**Eggs:** 4–5; white without markings

**Incubation:** 19–21 days; female and male incubate

**Fledging:** 28–30 days; female and male feed the young

**Migration:** complete, to South America

**Food:** insects caught in midair

**Compare:** The Purple Martin (p. 79) is much larger and darker. The Barn Swallow (p. 77) has a deeply forked tail. Look for the cigar shape to identify the Chimney Swift in flight.

**Stan's Notes:** One of the fastest fliers in the bird world. Spends all day flying, rarely perching. Flies in groups, feeding on insects flying 100 feet (30 m) or higher up in the air. Often called a Flying Cigar due to its body shape, which is pointed at both ends. Drinks and bathes during flight, skimming water. Gives a unique in-flight twittering call, often heard before the bird is seen. Hundreds roost in large chimneys, giving it the common name. Builds its nest with tiny twigs, cementing it with saliva and attaching it to the inside of a chimney or a hollow tree. Usually only one nest per chimney.

# Chipping Sparrow
*Spizella passerina*

SUMMER

**Size:** 5" (13 cm)

**Male:** Small gray-brown sparrow with clear-gray chest. Rusty crown. White eyebrows and thin, black eye line. Thin, gray-black bill. Two faint wing bars.

**Female:** same as male

**Juvenile:** similar to adults, with streaking on the chest; lacks a rusty crown

**Nest:** cup; female builds; 2 broods per year

**Eggs:** 3–5; blue-green with brown markings

**Incubation:** 11–14 days; female incubates

**Fledging:** 10–12 days; female and male feed the young

**Migration:** complete, to southern states, Mexico and Central America

**Food:** insects, seeds; will come to ground feeders

**Compare:** Similar to American Tree Sparrow (p. 109), which shares a rusty crown, but lacks dark eye line. The Lark Sparrow (p. 113) is larger and has a white chest and central spot. Song Sparrow (p. 103) and female House Finch (p. 91) have heavily streaked chests. Look for the rusty crown and black eye line to help identify the Chipping Sparrow.

**Stan's Notes:** A common garden or yard bird, often seen feeding on dropped seeds beneath feeders. Gathers in large family groups to feed in preparation for migration. Migrates at night in flocks of 20–30 birds. The common name comes from the male's fast "chip" call. Often is just called Chippy. Builds nest low in dense shrubs and almost always lines it with animal hair.

WINTER

# Pine Siskin
*Spinus pinus*

| | |
|---|---|
| **Size:** | 5" (13 cm) |
| **Male:** | Small brown finch with heavy streaking on the back, breast and belly. Yellow wing bars. Yellow at the base of tail. Thin bill. |
| **Female:** | similar to male, with less yellow |
| **Juvenile:** | similar to adult, with a light-yellow tinge over the breast and chin |
| **Nest:** | cup; female builds; 2 broods |
| **Eggs:** | 3–4; greenish blue with brown markings |
| **Incubation:** | 12–13 days; female incubates |
| **Fledging:** | 14–15 days; female and male feed the young |
| **Migration:** | irruptive; moves around the United States in search of food |
| **Food:** | seeds, insects; will come to seed feeders |
| **Compare:** | Female House Finch (p. 91) lacks any yellow. Female Purple Finch (p. 111) has bold white eyebrows. The female American Goldfinch (p. 301) has white wing bars. Look for the yellow wing bars to identify the Pine Siskin. |

**Stan's Notes:** Usually considered a winter finch, seen in flocks of up to 20 birds, often with other finch species. While it can be found throughout Missouri in heavy invasion years, it is absent in many winters. Will come to thistle feeders. Gives a series of high-pitched, wheezy calls. Also gives a wheezing twitter. Nests irregularly in Missouri, with nests often only a few feet apart. Breeds in small groups. Builds nest toward the end of coniferous branches, where needles are dense, helping to conceal. Male feeds the female during incubation. Juveniles lose the yellow tint by late summer of their first year.

male
p. 275

female

# House Finch
*Haemorhous mexicanus*

**YEAR-ROUND**

| | |
|---|---|
| **Size:** | 5" (13 cm) |
| **Female:** | Plain brown with heavy streaking on a white chest. |
| **Male:** | red-to-orange face, throat, chest and rump, streaked belly and wings, brown cap, brown marking behind the eyes |
| **Juvenile:** | similar to female |
| **Nest:** | cup, occasionally in a cavity; female builds; 2 broods per year |
| **Eggs:** | 4–5; pale blue, lightly marked |
| **Incubation:** | 12–14 days; female incubates |
| **Fledging:** | 15–19 days; female and male feed the young |
| **Migration:** | non-migrator to partial migrator; will move around to find food |
| **Food:** | seeds, fruit, leaf buds; visits seed feeders and feeders that offer grape jelly |
| **Compare:** | The female Purple Finch (p. 111) is very similar but has bold white eyebrows. Pine Siskin (p. 89) is similar but has yellow wing bars and a smaller bill. The female American Goldfinch (p. 301) has a clear chest. Look for the heavily streaked chest to help identify the female House Finch. |

**Stan's Notes:** A very social bird, visiting feeders in small flocks. Likes to nest in hanging flower baskets. Male sings a loud, cheerful warbling song. A native finch to the American Southwest and was introduced to Long Island, New York, from the western U.S. in the 1940s. Now found throughout the country. Suffers from a disease that causes the eyes to crust, resulting in blindness and death.

# House Wren
*Troglodytes aedon*

SUMMER

**Size:** 5" (13 cm)

**Male:** All-brown bird with lighter-brown markings on the wings and tail. Slightly curved brown bill. Often holds tail upward.

**Female:** same as male

**Juvenile:** same as adult

**Nest:** cavity; female and male line just about any nest cavity; 2 broods per year

**Eggs:** 4–6; tan with brown markings

**Incubation:** 10–13 days; female and male incubate

**Fledging:** 12–15 days; female and male feed the young

**Migration:** complete, to southern states and Mexico

**Food:** insects, spiders, snails

**Compare:** Carolina Wren (p. 95) is slightly larger and has prominent eyebrows. Look for House Wren's long, curved bill and long, upturned tail to differentiate it from sparrows.

**Stan's Notes:** A prolific songster. During the mating season, sings from dawn to dusk. Seen in brushy yards, parks and woodlands and along forest edges. Easily attracted to a nest box. In spring, the male chooses several prospective nesting cavities and places a few small twigs in each. The female inspects all of them and finishes constructing the nest in the cavity of her choice. She fills the cavity with short twigs and then lines a small depression at the back with pine needles and grass. She often has trouble fitting longer twigs through the entrance hole and tries many different directions and approaches until she is successful.

# Carolina Wren

*Thryothorus ludovicianus*

YEAR-ROUND

**Size:** 5½" (14 cm)

**Male:** Rusty-brown head and back with an orange-yellow chest and belly. White throat and a prominent white eye stripe. Short, stubby tail, often cocked up.

**Female:** same as male

**Juvenile:** same as adults

**Nest:** cavity; female and male build; 2 broods per year, sometimes 3

**Eggs:** 4–6; white, sometimes pink or creamy, with brown markings

**Incubation:** 12–14 days; female incubates

**Fledging:** 12–14 days; female and male feed the young

**Migration:** non-migrator

**Food:** insects, fruit, few seeds; visits suet feeders

**Compare:** House Wren (p. 93) is darker brown and lacks the bold white eye stripe.

**Stan's Notes:** Mates are long-term, staying together throughout the year in permanent territories. Sings year-round. The male is known to sing up to 40 song types, singing one song repeatedly before switching to another. The female also sings, resulting in duets. The male often takes over feeding the first brood while the female renests. Range expands northward in years with mild winters. Nests in birdhouses and in unusual places like mailboxes, bumpers or broken taillights of vehicles, or nearly any other cavity. Found in brushy yards or woodlands. Can be attracted to feeders with mealworms.

male
p. 215

female

# Dark-eyed Junco
## *Junco hyemalis*

WINTER

| | |
|---|---|
| **Size:** | 5½" (14 cm) |
| **Female:** | A plump, dark-eyed bird with a tan-to-brown chest, head and back. White belly. Ivory-to-pink bill. White outer tail feathers appear like a white V in flight. |
| **Male:** | round bird with gray plumage |
| **Juvenile:** | similar to female, with streaking on the breast and head |
| **Nest:** | cup; female and male build; 2 broods per year |
| **Eggs:** | 3–5; white with reddish-brown markings |
| **Incubation:** | 12–13 days; female incubates |
| **Fledging:** | 10–13 days; male and female feed the young |
| **Migration:** | complete, throughout the U.S., winters in Missouri |
| **Food:** | seeds, insects; visits ground and seed feeders |
| **Compare:** | Rarely confused with any other bird. Look for the ivory-to-pink bill and small flocks feeding beneath seed feeders to help identify the female Dark-eyed Junco. |

**Stan's Notes:** One of the most common birds in the state during winter. Adheres to a rigid social hierarchy, with dominant birds chasing the less dominant birds. Look for the white outer tail feathers flashing in flight. Often seen in small flocks on the ground, where it uses its feet to simultaneously "double-scratch" to expose seeds and insects. Eats many weed seeds. Several junco species have now been combined into one, simply called Dark-eyed Junco. Nests in a wide variety of wooded habitats. Doesn't nest in Missouri.

female

male
p. 71

# Indigo Bunting
*Passerina cyanea*

| | |
|---|---|
| **Size:** | 5½" (14 cm) |
| **Female:** | Light-brown, finch-like bird. Faint streaking a light-tan chest. Wings have a very faint blue cast and indistinct wing bars. |
| **Male:** | vibrant blue with scattered dark markings on wings and tail |
| **Juvenile:** | similar to female |
| **Nest:** | cup; female builds; 2 broods per year |
| **Eggs:** | 3–4; pale blue without markings |
| **Incubation:** | 12–13 days; female incubates |
| **Fledging:** | 10–11 days; female feeds the young |
| **Migration:** | complete, to Mexico, Central America and South America |
| **Food:** | insects, seeds, fruit; will visit seed feeders |
| **Compare:** | Female Blue Grosbeak (p. 73) is larger and has 2 tan wing bars. The female House Finch (p. 91) has a heavily streaked chest. Female American Goldfinch (p. 301) has white wing bars. Look for the faint blue cast on the wings to help identify the female Indigo Bunting. |

**Stan's Notes:** Seen along woodland edges and in parks and yards, feeding on insects. Comes to seed feeders early in spring, before insects are plentiful. Secretive, plain and quiet; usually only the males are noticed. The male often sings from treetops to attract a mate. Migrates at night in flocks of 5–10 birds. Males return before the females and juveniles, often to the nest site of the preceding year. Juveniles move to within a mile of their birth site.

# Cliff Swallow
*Petrochelidon pyrrhonota*

SUMMER

**Size:** 5½" (14 cm)

**Male:** Uniquely patterned swallow with a dark b..
wings and cap. Distinctive tan-to-rust rump,
cheeks and forehead.

**Female:** same as male

**Juvenile:** similar to adult, lacks distinct patterning

**Nest:** gourd-shaped, made of mud; male and
female build; 1–2 broods per year

**Eggs:** 4–6; pale white with brown markings

**Incubation:** 14–16 days; male and female incubate

**Fledging:** 21–24 days; female and male feed young

**Migration:** complete, to South America

**Food:** insects

**Compare:** Barn Swallow (p. 77) is larger and has a
distinctive, deeply forked tail and blue
back and wings.

**Stan's Notes:** A common and widespread swallow in the state.
Common around bridges (especially bridges over water) and rural
housing (especially in open country near cliffs). Builds a gourd-
shaped nest with a funnel-like entrance pointing down. A colony
nester, with many nests lined up beneath building eaves or cliff
overhangs. Will carry balls of mud up to a mile to construct its
nest. Many in the colony return to the same nest site each year.
Not unusual to have two broods per season. If the number of
nests underneath eaves becomes a problem, wait until the young
have left the nests to hose off the mud.

# Song Sparrow
*Melospiza melodia*

**YEAR-ROUND WINTER**

**Size:** 5–6" (13–15 cm)

**Male:** Common brown sparrow with heavy dark streaks on the chest coalescing into a central dark spot.

**Female:** same as male

**Juvenile:** similar to adults, with a finely streaked chest; lacks a central dark spot

**Nest:** cup; female builds; 2 broods per year

**Eggs:** 3–4; blue to green, with red-brown markings

**Incubation:** 12–14 days; female incubates

**Fledging:** 9–12 days; female and male feed the young

**Migration:** complete, to southern states; non-migrator in most of Missouri

**Food:** insects, seeds; only rarely comes to ground feeders with seeds

**Compare:** Similar to other brown sparrows. Look for the heavily streaked chest with a central dark spot to help identify the Song Sparrow.

**Stan's Notes:** There are many subspecies of this bird, but the dark spot in the center of the chest appears in every variety. A constant songster, repeating its loud, clear song every few minutes. The song varies from region to region but has the same basic structure. Sings from thick shrubs to defend a small territory, beginning with three notes and finishing up with a trill. A ground feeder, it will "double-scratch" with both feet at the same time to expose seeds. When the female builds a new nest for a second brood, the male often takes over feeding the first brood. Unlike many other sparrow species, Song Sparrows rarely flock together. A common host of the Brown-headed Cowbird.

# House Sparrow
*Passer domesticus*

**YEAR-ROUND**

**Size:** 6" (15 cm)

**Male:** Brown back with a gray belly and cap. Large black patch extending from the throat to the chest (bib). One white wing bar.

**Female:** slightly smaller than the male; light brown with light eyebrows; lacks a bib and white wing bar

**Juvenile:** similar to female

**Nest:** cavity; female and male build a domed cup nest within; 2–3 broods per year

**Eggs:** 4–6; white with brown markings

**Incubation:** 10–12 days; female incubates

**Fledging:** 14–17 days; female and male feed the young

**Migration:** non-migrator; moves around to find food

**Food:** seeds, insects, fruit; comes to seed feeders

**Compare:** Eurasian Tree Sparrow (p. 105) has a black ear patch. Harris's Sparrow (p. 135) has a black "hood" and white breast. American Tree Sparrow (p. 109) and Chipping Sparrow (p. 87) both have rusty-red crowns.

**Stan's Notes:** One of the first birdsongs heard in cities in spring. A familiar city bird, nearly always in small flocks. Also found on farms. Introduced in 1850 from Europe to Central Park in New York. Now seen throughout North America. Related to old-world sparrows; not a relative of any sparrows in the U.S. An aggressive bird that will kill young birds in order to take over the nest cavity. Uses dried grass and small scraps of plastic, paper and other materials to build an oversize, domed nest in the cavity.

# American Tree Sparrow
*Spizelloides arborea*

WINTER

**Size:** 6" (15 cm)

**Male:** Brown with a tan chest and rusty crown and eye line. Gray eyebrows. Dark spot in the center of the chest. Dark upper bill; yellow lower bill. 2 white wing bars.

**Female:** same as male

**Juvenile:** streaked chest often obscures the central dark spot; lacks a rusty crown

**Nest:** cup; female builds; 1 brood per year

**Eggs:** 3–5; greenish white with brown markings

**Incubation:** 12–13 days; female incubates

**Fledging:** 8–10 days; female and male feed the young

**Migration:** complete, across North America; winters in Missouri

**Food:** insects, seeds; visits seed feeders

**Compare:** The Chipping Sparrow (p. 87) has white eyebrows and a black eye line. The Song Sparrow (p. 103) has a heavily streaked chest. To identify the American Tree Sparrow, check for the dark spot on the chest and the two-toned bill.

**Stan's Notes:** Commonly seen during spring and fall migrations in flocks of 2–200 birds. A regular winter bird feeder visitor in Missouri. Found in open fields, woodlands and suburban backyards. Sometimes called a Winter Chippy because it looks like the Chipping Sparrow. Gives a series of high-pitched, sweet-sounding whistles. Nests in Canada and Alaska. The species name *arborea* means "tree," but it doesn't nest in trees; it nests on the ground in a clump of grass. The "Tree" in the name refers to its habitat. "American" refers to its natural range.

male
p. 277

female

# Purple Finch
*Haemorhous purpureus*

WINTER

| | |
|---|---|
| **Size:** | 6" (15 cm) |
| **Female:** | Plain brown with heavy streaking on the chest. Bold white eyebrows and a large bill. |
| **Male:** | raspberry-red head, cap, breast, back and rump; brownish wings and tail |
| **Juvenile:** | same as female |
| **Nest:** | cup; female and male build; 1 brood per year |
| **Eggs:** | 4–5; greenish blue with brown markings |
| **Incubation:** | 12–13 days; female incubates |
| **Fledging:** | 13–14 days; female and male feed the young |
| **Migration:** | irruptive; moves around in search of food |
| **Food:** | seeds, insects, fruit; comes to seed feeders |
| **Compare:** | The female House Finch (p. 91) lacks eyebrows. The Pine Siskin (p. 89) has yellow wing bars. The female American Goldfinch (p. 301) has a clear chest. Look for the bold white eyebrows to identify the female Purple Finch. |

**Stan's Notes:** Usually seen only during the migration and in winter, when flocks of Purple Finches leave their homes farther north and move around searching for food. Travels in flocks of up to 50 birds. Visits seed feeders along with House Finches, which makes it hard to tell them apart. Feeds mainly on seeds; ash tree seeds are an important source of food. Found in coniferous forests, mixed woods, woodland edges and suburban backyards. Flies in the typical undulating, up-and-down pattern of finches. Sings a rich, loud song. Gives a distinctive "tic" note only in flight. The male is not purple. The Latin species name *purpureus* means "purple" (and other reddish colors).

# Lark Sparrow
*Chondestes grammacus*

SUMMER

**Size:** 6½" (16 cm)

**Male:** All-brown bird with unique rust-red, white and black head pattern. A white breast with a central black spot. Gray rump and white edges to gray tail, as seen in flight.

**Female:** same as male

**Juvenile:** similar to adult, but no rust-red on head

**Nest:** cup, on the ground; female builds; 1 brood per year

**Eggs:** 3–6; pale white with brown markings

**Incubation:** 10–12 days; male and female incubate

**Fledging:** 10–12 days; female and male feed young

**Migration:** complete, to coastal Mexico, Central America

**Food:** seeds, insects

**Compare:** The White-throated Sparrow (p. 115) and the White-crowned Sparrow (p. 117) both lack the Lark Sparrow's rust-red pattern on the head and central spot on a white chest. Chipping Sparrow (p. 87) has a similar rusty color on head, but it is smaller and lacks Lark Sparrow's white breast and central spot.

**Stan's Notes:** One of the larger sparrow species and one of the best songsters, also well known for its courtship strutting, chasing and lark-like flight pattern (rapid wingbeats with tail spread). A bird of open fields, pastures and prairies, found almost anywhere. Very common during migration, when large flocks congregate. Will use nest for several years if first brood is successful.

# White-throated Sparrow
*Zonotrichia albicollis*

WINTER

**Size:** 6–7" (15–18 cm)

**Male:** Brown with a gray or tan chest and belly. White or tan throat patch and eyebrows. Bold striping on the head. Small yellow spot in the space between the eye and bill, called the lore.

**Female:** same as male

**Juvenile:** similar to adults, with a heavily streaked chest and a gray throat and eyebrows

**Nest:** cup; female builds; 1 brood per year

**Eggs:** 4–6; green to blue, or cream-white with red-brown markings

**Incubation:** 11–14 days; female incubates

**Fledging:** 10–12 days; female and male feed the young

**Migration:** complete, to southern states and Mexico

**Food:** insects, seeds, fruit; visits ground feeders

**Compare:** The White-crowned Sparrow (p. 117) lacks throat patch and yellow lore. Lark Sparrow (p. 113) has a rust-red pattern on the head and central black spot on a white chest.

**Stan's Notes:** Two color variations (polymorphic): white-striped and tan-striped. Studies indicate white-striped adults tend to mate with tan-striped birds; not clear why. Winter resident that is more abundant during migration, when it can be seen at ground feeders. Known for its wonderful song; it sings all year and can be heard at night. White- and tan-striped males and white-striped females sing, but tan-striped females do not. Builds nest on the ground under small trees in bogs and coniferous forests. Immature and first-year females tend to winter farther south than adults.

juvenile

WINTER

# White-crowned Sparrow
*Zonotrichia leucophrys*

**Size:** 6½–7½" (16.5–19 cm)

**Male:** Brown with a gray chest and black-and-white striped crown. Small, thin, pink bill.

**Female:** same as male

**Juvenile:** similar to adults, with black and brown stripes on the head

**Nest:** cup; female builds; 2 broods per year

**Eggs:** 3–5; greenish to bluish to whitish with red-brown markings

**Incubation:** 11–14 days; female incubates

**Fledging:** 8–12 days; male and female feed the young

**Migration:** complete, to southern states and Mexico; winters in Missouri

**Food:** insects, seeds, berries; visits ground feeders

**Compare:** The White-throated Sparrow (p. 115) has a white or tan throat patch, and yellow spot between the eyes and bill, with a blackish bill. Lark Sparrow (p. 113) has a rust-red pattern on the head and a central black spot on a white breast. Look for the striped crown to help identify the White-crowned Sparrow.

**Stan's Notes:** Often in groups of up to 20 birds during migration and winter. This ground feeder will "double-scratch" backward with both feet simultaneously to find seeds. The males are prolific songsters, singing in late winter while migrating north. Males arrive at the breeding grounds before the females and sing from perches to establish territory. Males take most of the responsibility for raising the young while females start their second broods. Only 9–12 days separate the broods. Doesn't nest in Missouri.

# Fox Sparrow
*Passerella iliaca*

WINTER

**Size:** 7" (18 cm)

**Male:** Plump, rust-red sparrow. Heavily streaked, rusty breast and solid-rust tail. Head and back are mottled with gray.

**Female:** same as male

**Juvenile:** same as adults

**Nest:** cup; female builds; 2 broods per year

**Eggs:** 2–4; pale green with reddish markings

**Incubation:** 12–14 days; female incubates

**Fledging:** 10–11 days; female and male feed the young

**Migration:** complete, to southern states; winters in Missouri

**Food:** seeds, insects; comes to ground feeders

**Compare:** The Brown Thrasher (p. 157) is much larger, is slimmer and has a long, curved bill. The rust-red plumage of the Fox Sparrow differentiates it from all other sparrows.

**Stan's Notes:** One of the largest sparrows. Often seen alone or in small groups. Found in shrubby areas, open fields and backyards. Comes to ground feeders; searches for seeds and insects underneath seed feeders during migration and winter. Like a chicken, it will "double-scratch" with both feet at the same time to look for food. Gives a series of rich notes lasting 2–3 seconds, usually singing from a perch hidden in a shrub. The common name "Sparrow" comes from the Anglo-Saxon word *spearwa*, meaning "flutterer," as applies to any small bird. "Fox" refers to its rusty color. Appears in several color variations, depending on location. Nests on the ground in brush and along forest edges in Canada and Alaska.

MIGRATION

# Swainson's Thrush
*Catharus ustulatus*

**Size:** 7" (18 cm)

**Male:** Dusty-brown head, back and wings. Brown smudges and spots, especially beneath chin, on the chest and on an off-white belly. Small, thin, two-toned bill, yellow under and black above.

**Female:** same as male

**Juvenile:** similar to adult, less distinct spots on chest

**Nest:** cup; female builds; 1 brood per year

**Eggs:** 3–5; pale blue with brown markings

**Incubation:** 12–14 days; female incubates

**Fledging:** 10–14 days; female and male feed young

**Migration:** complete, to Mexico, Central America and South America

**Food:** insects, fruit

**Compare:** American Robin (p. 231) is similar in shape, but it is larger and has a red breast and a gray head and back.

**Stan's Notes:** A common thrush during spring and fall migrations. Often hard to see because most of the time it stays on the ground in thick vegetation. Feeds mostly on insects in spring and summer, adding fruit to its diet in late summer. Nests in shrubs or low in conifer trees, building a bulky cup nest consisting of grass, bark and moss, all glued together with mud. Doesn't nest in Missouri.

male
p. 73

female

# Blue Grosbeak
*Passerina caerulea*

SUMMER

| | |
|---|---|
| **Size:** | 7" (18 cm) |
| **Female:** | Overall brown with darker wings and tail. Two tan wing bars. Large gray-to-silver bill. |
| **Male:** | blue bird with 2 chestnut wing bars; large gray-to-silver bill; black around base of bill |
| **Juvenile:** | similar to female |
| **Nest:** | cup; female builds; 1–2 broods per year |
| **Eggs:** | 3–6; pale blue without markings |
| **Incubation:** | 11–12 days; female incubates |
| **Fledging:** | 9–10 days; female and male feed the young |
| **Migration:** | complete, to Mexico and Central America |
| **Food:** | insects, seeds; will come to seed feeders |
| **Compare:** | The female Indigo Bunting (p. 99) is very similar, but it is smaller, more common, lacks the tan wing bars and is lighter in color overall. |

**Stan's Notes:** Found throughout Missouri. A bird of semi-open habitats such as overgrown fields, riversides, woodland edges and fencerows. Visits seed feeders, where it can be confused with female Indigo Buntings. Often seen twitching and spreading its tail. The first-year males show only some blue, obtaining the full complement of blue feathers in the second winter. It has expanded northward, and its overall populations have increased over the past 30–40 years.

male
p. 49

female

# Rose-breasted Grosbeak
*Pheucticus ludovicianus*

**SUMMER MIGRATION**

**Size:** 7–8" (18–20 cm)

**Female:** Plump and heavily streaked. Large, obvious white eyebrows. Large ivory bill. Orange-to-yellow wing linings.

**Male:** black-and-white with a triangular rose patch in the center of chest, rose-red wing linings

**Juvenile:** similar to female

**Nest:** cup; female and male construct; 1–2 broods per year

**Eggs:** 3–5; blue-green with brown markings

**Incubation:** 13–14 days; female and male incubate

**Fledging:** 9–12 days; female and male feed the young

**Migration:** complete, to Mexico, Central America and South America

**Food:** insects, seeds, fruit; comes to seed feeders

**Compare:** Looks like a large finch with bold white eyebrows and heavy streaking. Female Purple Finch (p. 111) has smaller eyebrows. Female House Finch (p. 91) lacks eyebrows.

**Stan's Notes:** Most common in hardwood forests in the northern half of Missouri. Seen in small groups. Prefers a mature deciduous forest for nesting. Both sexes sing, but the male sings much louder and clearer. Sings a rich, robin-like song with a chip note in the tune. "Grosbeak" refers to the thick, strong bill, which is used to crush seeds. Males arrive at the breeding grounds a few days before females. Several males will visit seed feeders together in spring. After fledging, young grosbeaks visit feeders with adults. Makes short flights from tree to tree with rapid wingbeats. Late to arrive in spring and early to leave in autumn.

female

male
p. 25

# Eastern Towhee
*Pipilo erythrophthalmus*

**YEAR-ROUND**
**SUMMER**

**Size:** 7–8" (18–20 cm)

**Female:** A mostly light-brown bird. Rusty red-brown sides and a white belly. Long, brown tail with a white tip. Short, stout, pointed bill and rich red eyes. White wing patches flash in flight.

**Male:** similar to female, but black instead of brown

**Juvenile:** light brown with heavily streaked head, chest and belly, a long, dark tail with a white tip

**Nest:** cup; female builds; 2 broods per year

**Eggs:** 3–4; cream-white with brown markings

**Incubation:** 12–13 days; female incubates

**Fledging:** 10–12 days; male and female feed young

**Migration:** complete to non-migrator, to southern states, South America; non-migrator in much of Missouri

**Food:** insects, seeds, fruit; visits ground feeders

**Compare:** American Robin (p. 231) is larger, and it has a red breast and lacks the white belly. The female Rose-breasted Grosbeak (p. 125) has a heavily streaked breast and obvious white eyebrows.

**Stan's Notes:** Named for its distinctive "tow-hee" call, given by both sexes. Known mostly for its other characteristic call, which sounds like "drink-your-tea!" Will hop backward with both feet (bilateral scratching), raking up leaf litter to locate insects and seeds. The female does the brooding. Male feeds the young most of the time. White-eyed form in southern states, red-eyed elsewhere.

female

male

# Horned Lark
*Eremophila alpestris*

**YEAR-ROUND**

**Size:** 7–8" (18-20 cm)

**Male:** Tan to brown with black markings on the face. Black necklace and bill. Pale-yellow chin. Two tiny feather "horns" on the top of the head, sometimes hard to see. Dark tail with white outer tail feathers, seen in flight.

**Female:** duller than male; less noticeable "horns"

**Juvenile:** lacks a yellow chin and black markings; does not develop "horns" until the second year

**Nest:** ground; female builds; 2–3 broods per year

**Eggs:** 3–4; gray with brown markings

**Incubation:** 11–12 days; female incubates

**Fledging:** 9–12 days; female and male feed the young

**Migration:** non-migrator to partial in Missouri

**Food:** seeds, insects

**Compare:** The Eastern Meadowlark (p. 319) has a yellow breast and belly. Look for the black markings by the eyes and the black necklace to identify the Horned Lark.

**Stan's Notes:** The only true lark native to North America. A bird of open ground. Common in rural areas; often seen in large flocks. The population increased in North America over the past century as more land was cleared for farming. Male performs a fluttering courtship flight high in the air while singing a high-pitched song. Female performs a fluttering distraction display when the nest is disturbed. Starts breeding early in the year. Able to renest about a week after the brood fledges. Moves around in winter to find food. "Lark" comes from the Middle English *laverock*, or "a lark."

male
p. 27

female

# Brown-headed Cowbird

*Molothrus ater*

**YEAR-ROUND**

| | |
|---|---|
| **Size:** | 7½" (19 cm) |
| **Female:** | Dull brown with no obvious markings. Pointed, sharp, gray bill. Dark eyes. |
| **Male:** | glossy black with a chocolate-brown head |
| **Juvenile:** | similar to female but with dull-gray plumage and a streaked chest |
| **Nest:** | no nest; lays eggs in the nests of other birds |
| **Eggs:** | 5–7; white with brown markings |
| **Incubation:** | 10–13 days; host bird incubates the eggs |
| **Fledging:** | 10–11 days; host birds feed the young |
| **Migration:** | non-migrator in Missouri; moves around to find food in winter |
| **Food:** | insects, seeds; will come to seed feeders |
| **Compare:** | The female Red-winged Blackbird (p. 143) has white eyebrows and heavy streaking. The female Indigo Bunting (p. 99) has faint blue on its wings. The pointed gray bill helps to identify the female Brown-headed Cowbird. |

**Stan's Notes:** Cowbirds are members of the blackbird family. Of approximately 750 species of parasitic birds worldwide, this is the only parasitic bird in Missouri. Brood parasites lay their eggs in the nests of other birds, leaving the host birds to raise their young. Cowbirds are known to have laid their eggs in the nests of over 200 species of birds. While some birds reject cowbird eggs, most incubate them and raise the young, even to the exclusion of their own. Look for warblers and other birds feeding young birds twice their own size. Named "Cowbird" for its habit of following bison and cattle herds to feed on insects flushed up by the animals.

1 year old

Bohemian Waxwing

# Cedar Waxwing
## *Bombycilla cedrorum*

**YEAR-ROUND**

| | |
|---|---|
| **Size:** | 7½" (19 cm) |
| **Male:** | Sleek-looking, gray-to-brown bird. Pointed crest, bandit-like mask and light-yellow belly. Bold-yellow tip of tail. Red wing tips look like they were dipped in red wax. |
| **Female:** | same as male |
| **Juvenile:** | grayish with a heavily streaked breast; lacks the sleek look, black mask and red wing tips |
| **Nest:** | cup; female and male construct; 1 brood per year, occasionally 2 |
| **Eggs:** | 4–6; pale blue with brown markings |
| **Incubation:** | 10–12 days; female incubates |
| **Fledging:** | 14–18 days; female and male feed the young |
| **Migration:** | partial migrator; moves around to find food |
| **Food:** | cedar cones, fruit, insects |
| **Compare:** | Similar to its larger, less common cousin, Bohemian Waxwing (see inset). Look for the red wing tips, yellow-tipped tail and black mask to identify the Cedar Waxwing. |

**Stan's Notes:** The name is derived from its red, wax-like wing tips and preference for the small, berry-like cones of the cedar. Seen in flocks, moving around from area to area looking for berries. Feeds on insects during summer, before berries are abundant. Wanders during winter, searching for food supplies. Spends most of its time at the top of tall trees. Listen for the high-pitched "sreee" whistling sound it constantly makes while perched or in flight. Obtains the mask after the first year and red wing tips after the second year.

# Harris's Sparrow
*Zonotrichia querula*

MIGRATION
WINTER

**Size:** 7½" (19 cm)

**Male:** A very large sparrow with various amounts of black on head, extending down the nape and face onto the chest. White belly. Brown back and wings. Pink bill and legs.

**Female:** same as male

**Juvenile:** similar to adult, lacks the black "hood" and spotted chest

**Nest:** cup, on the ground; unknown who builds; 1 brood per year

**Eggs:** 4–5; white with brown markings

**Incubation:** 13–14 days; female incubates

**Fledging:** 11–12 days; female and male feed young

**Migration:** complete, to central states; winters in Missouri

**Food:** insects, seeds, berries, ground feeders

**Compare:** House Sparrow (p. 107) lacks the Harris's black "hood."

**Stan's Notes:** A large sparrow commonly seen in small groups of up to ten birds scratching under seed feeders during spring and fall migrations. Nests in northern Canada, returning to the western portion of Missouri and central U.S. for the winter. Recent studies show that a bird's status is dependent upon the amount of black on its "hood," not its age. The more black, the higher the status. Named after Edward Harris (1799-1863), a companion of John James Audubon.

# Wood Thrush
*Hylocichla mustelina*

SUMMER

**Size:** 8" (20 cm)

**Male:** Reddish-brown head, back and wings with color fading into a brown tail. A distinctive white breast, belly and sides, covered with black spots. White ring around black eyes, obvious on a black-streaked white face.

**Female:** same as male

**Juvenile:** similar to adult

**Nest:** cup; female builds; 1–2 broods per year

**Eggs:** 2–4; greenish blue without markings

**Incubation:** 13–14 days; female incubates

**Fledging:** 11–12 days; female and male feed the young

**Migration:** complete, to Central and South America

**Food:** insects, fruit

**Compare:** American Robin (p. 231) has a similar body shape, but it has a red breast. Brown Thrasher (p. 157) is a similar rusty color, but it has a much longer rusty-red tail and bright-yellow eyes in comparison to the shorter brown tail and black eyes of Wood Thrush.

**Stan's Notes:** An easy thrush to identify due to the large dark spots on breast and belly. Well known for its liquid flute-like calls, heard deep within woodlots throughout Missouri. Returns to the same woodlands during the last two weeks of March. Often seen on the ground, hopping around like a robin in search of insects.

1

winter

breeding

# Spotted Sandpiper
*Actitis macularius*

SUMMER

**Size:** 8" (20 cm)

**Male:** Olive-brown back with black spots on a white chest and belly. White line over eyes. Long, dull-yellow legs. Long bill. Winter plumage lacks spots on the chest and belly.

**Female:** same as male

**Juvenile:** similar to winter plumage, with a darker bill

**Nest:** ground; male builds; 2 broods per year

**Eggs:** 3–4; brownish with brown markings

**Incubation:** 20–24 days; male incubates

**Fledging:** 17–21 days; male feeds the young

**Migration:** complete migrator, to southern states, Mexico, Central and South America

**Food:** aquatic insects

**Compare:** Lesser Yellowlegs (p. 153) is larger. Killdeer (p. 155) has 2 black neck bands. Look for the black spots on the chest and belly and the bobbing tail to help identify the breeding Spotted Sandpiper.

**Stan's Notes:** This is one of the more common sandpipers. Seen along the shorelines of large ponds, lakes and rivers. One of the few shorebirds that will dive underwater when pursued. Able to fly straight up out of the water. Holds wings in a cup-like arc in flight, rarely lifting them above a horizontal plane. Walks as if delicately balanced. When standing, constantly bobs its tail. Gives a rapid series of "weet-weet-weet" calls when frightened and flying away. Female mates with multiple males and lays eggs in up to five nests. Male does all of the nest building, incubating and childcare without any help from the female.

male
p. 283

female

juvenile

# Northern Cardinal
*Cardinalis cardinalis*

YEAR-ROUND

| | |
|---|---|
| **Size:** | 8–9" (20–23 cm) |
| **Female:** | Buff-brown with red tinges on the crest and wings. Black mask and a large reddish bill. |
| **Male:** | red with a large crest and bill and a black mask extending from the face to the throat |
| **Juvenile:** | same as female but with a blackish-gray bill |
| **Nest:** | cup; female builds; 2–3 broods per year |
| **Eggs:** | 3–4; bluish white with brown markings |
| **Incubation:** | 12–13 days; female and male incubate |
| **Fledging:** | 9–10 days; female and male feed the young |
| **Migration:** | non-migrator |
| **Food:** | seeds, insects, fruit; comes to seed feeders |
| **Compare:** | The Cedar Waxwing (p. 133) has a small, dark bill. The juvenile Northern Cardinal (bottom inset) looks like the adult female but with a dark bill. Look for the reddish bill to identify the female Northern Cardinal. |

**Stan's Notes:** A familiar backyard bird. Seen in a variety of habitats, including parks. Usually likes thick vegetation. One of the few species in which both females and males sing. Can be heard all year. Listen for its "whata-cheer-cheer-cheer" territorial call in spring. Watch for a male feeding a female during courtship. The male also feeds the young of the first brood while the female builds a second nest. Territorial in spring, fighting its own reflection in a window or other reflective surface. Non-territorial in winter, gathering in small flocks of up to 20 birds. Makes short flights from cover to cover, often landing on the ground. *Cardinalis* denotes importance, as represented by the red priestly garments of Catholic cardinals.

male
p. 31

female

# Red-winged Blackbird

*Agelaius phoeniceus*

| | |
|---:|:---|
| **Size:** | 8½" (22 cm) |
| **Female:** | Heavily streaked brown body. Pointed brown bill and white eyebrows. |
| **Male:** | jet black with red-and-yellow shoulder patches (epaulets) and a pointed black bill |
| **Juvenile:** | same as female |
| **Nest:** | cup; female builds; 2–3 broods per year |
| **Eggs:** | 3–4; bluish green with brown markings |
| **Incubation:** | 10–12 days; female incubates |
| **Fledging:** | 11–14 days; female and male feed the young |
| **Migration:** | non-migrator to partial migrator |
| **Food:** | seeds, insects; visits seed and suet feeders |
| **Compare:** | Female Brown-headed Cowbird (p. 131) is smaller and female Yellow-headed Blackbird (p. 149) is larger, both of which lack white eyebrows and streaks on chest. Thinner body than female Rose-breasted Grosbeak (p. 125) and has a pointed bill. |

**Stan's Notes:** One of the most widespread and numerous birds in the state. Found around marshes, wetlands, lakes and rivers. Flocks with as many as 10,000 birds have been reported. Males arrive before females and sing to defend their territory. The male repeats his call from the top of a cattail while showing off his red-and-yellow shoulder patches. The female chooses a mate and often builds her nest over shallow water in a thick stand of cattails. The male can be aggressive when defending the nest. Feeds mostly on seeds in spring and fall, and insects throughout the summer.

female

male

SUMMER

# Common Nighthawk
*Chordeiles minor*

**Size:** 9" (23 cm)

**Male:** Camouflaged brown and white with a white chin. Distinctive white band across the wings and tail, seen only in flight.

**Female:** similar to male, with a tan chin; lacks a white tail band

**Juvenile:** similar to female

**Nest:** no nest; lays eggs on the ground, usually on rocks, or on rooftop; 1 brood per year

**Eggs:** 2; cream with lavender markings

**Incubation:** 19–20 days; female and male incubate

**Fledging:** 20–21 days; female and male feed the young

**Migration:** complete, to South America

**Food:** insects caught in the air

**Compare:** The Chimney Swift (p. 85) is much smaller. Look for the white chin, obvious white band on the wings and characteristic flap-flap-flap-glide pattern to help identify the Common Nighthawk.

**Stan's Notes:** Usually only seen in flight at dusk or after sunset but not uncommon to see it sleeping on a branch during the day. A prolific insect eater and very noisy in flight, repeating a "peenting" call. Alternates slow wingbeats with bursts of quick wingbeats. In cities, prefers to nest on flat rooftops with gravel. City populations are on the decline as gravel rooftops are converted to other styles. In spring, the male performs a showy mating ritual consisting of a steep diving flight ending with a loud popping noise. One of the first birds to migrate in fall, starting in August. Often seen in large flocks.

in flight

juvenile

male

female

in-flight
juvenile

# American Kestrel
*Falco sparverius*

**YEAR-ROUND**

| | |
|---|---|
| **Size:** | 9–11" (23–28 cm); up to 2' wingspan |
| **Male:** | Rust-brown back and tail. White breast with dark spots. Two vertical black lines on a white face. Blue-gray wings. Wide black band with a white edge on the tip of a rusty tail. |
| **Female:** | similar to male but slightly larger, with rust-brown wings and dark bands on the tail |
| **Juvenile:** | same as adult of the same sex |
| **Nest:** | cavity; does not build a nest; 1 brood per year |
| **Eggs:** | 4–5; white with brown markings |
| **Incubation:** | 29–31 days; male and female incubate |
| **Fledging:** | 30–31 days; female and male feed the young |
| **Migration:** | non-migrator to partial migrator; moves around to find food in winter |
| **Food:** | insects, small mammals and birds, reptiles |
| **Compare:** | The Peregrine Falcon (p. 245) is much larger and has a dark "hood" marking. No other small bird of prey has a rusty back and tail. |

**Stan's Notes:** An unusual raptor because the sexes look different (dimorphic). Due to its small size, this falcon was once called a Sparrow Hawk. Hovers near roads, then dives for prey. Watch for it to pump its tail after landing on a perch. Perches nearly upright. Eats many grasshoppers. Adapts quickly to a wooden nest box. Can be extremely vocal, giving a loud series of high-pitched calls. Ability to see ultraviolet (UV) light helps it locate mice and other prey by their urine, which glows bright yellow in UV light.

male
p. 33

female

# Yellow-headed Blackbird

*Xanthocephalus xanthocephalus*

SUMMER
MIGRATION

**Size:** 9–11" (23–28 cm)

**Female:** Large brown bird with a dull-yellow head and chest. Slightly smaller than the male.

**Male:** black bird with a lemon-yellow head, breast and nape of neck, black mask, gray bill and white wing patches

**Juvenile:** similar to female

**Nest:** cup; female builds; 2 broods per year

**Eggs:** 3–5; greenish white with brown markings

**Incubation:** 11–13 days; female incubates

**Fledging:** 9–12 days; female feeds the young

**Migration:** complete, to southern states and Mexico

**Food:** insects, seeds; will come to ground feeders

**Compare:** Female Red-winged Blackbird (p. 143) is smaller and has white eyebrows and heavy streaking. Look for the dull-yellow head to help identify the female Yellow-headed.

**Stan's Notes:** Found around marshes, wetlands, and lakes. Nests in deep water, unlike its cousin, the Red-winged Blackbird, which prefers shallow water. Usually heard before seen. Gives a raspy, low, metallic-sounding call. The male is the only large black bird with a bright-yellow head. He gives an impressive mating display, flying with his head drooped and feet and tail pointing down while steadily beating his wings. Young keep low and out of sight for up to three weeks before they start to fly. Migrates in large flocks of as many as 200 birds, often with Red-winged Blackbirds and Brown-headed Cowbirds. Flocks of mainly males return in late March and early April; females return later. Most colonies consist of 20–100 nests.

male

female

# Northern Bobwhite
*Colinus virginianus*

YEAR-ROUND

**Size:** 10" (25 cm)

**Male:** Short, stocky and mostly brown with short, gray tail. Prominent white eye stripe and white chin. Reddish-brown sides and belly, often with black lines and dots.

**Female:** similar to male, with buff-brown eye stripe and chin

**Juvenile:** smaller and duller than adults

**Nest:** ground; female and male construct; 1 brood per year

**Eggs:** 12–15; white to creamy without markings

**Incubation:** 23–24 days; female and male incubate

**Fledging:** 6–7 days; female and male feed the young

**Migration:** non-migrator

**Food:** insects, seeds, fruit; will come to ground feeders offering corn and millet

**Compare:** Greater Prairie-Chicken (p. 177) is larger and lacks Bobwhite's prominent white eye stripe, and reddish-brown sides and belly.

**Stan's Notes:** Prefers shrubs, orchards, hedgerows and pastures. Moves around in small flocks of 20 birds (often family members), called a covey. The covey often rests together during the night, in a tight circle with tails together and heads facing outward, to watch for predators. Males and females perform distraction displays when nests or young are threatened. Nest is a depression in the ground lined with grass. Often pulls nearby vegetation over nest to help conceal it. Male gives a rising whistle, "bob-white," heard mainly in spring and summer. Also gives a single "hoy" call year-round.

# Lesser Yellowlegs
*Tringa flavipes*

MIGRATION

**Size:** 10–12" (25–30 cm)

**Male:** A typical sandpiper-type bird with a brown back and wings. Streaked white chest. Thin, straight black bill. Long, yellow legs.

**Female:** same as male

**Juvenile:** same as adult

**Nest:** ground; female builds; 1 brood per year

**Eggs:** 3–4; yellowish with brown markings

**Incubation:** 22–23 days; male and female incubate

**Fledging:** 18–20 days; male and female lead the young to food

**Migration:** complete, to Mexico, Central America and South America

**Food:** aquatic insects, tiny fish

**Compare:** The breeding Spotted Sandpiper (p. 139) has black spots on its chest. Look for the straight black bill and long, yellow legs of Lesser Yellowlegs.

**Stan's Notes:** Often seen in small flocks, combing shorelines and mudflats in search of food. Usually walks with its head down and tail up, ready to snatch up prey. Uses its long, straight bill to pluck insects and tiny fish out of the water. A member of the sandpiper group known as Tattlers, which scream alarm calls when taking off. Quite often moves into the water before taking flight, and gives a variety of flight notes at takeoff. Nest is a simple depression atop a mound of earth. Nests in marshes in the spruce forests of central Alaska and Canada.

# Killdeer
*Charadrius vociferus*

**YEAR-ROUND SUMMER**

**Size:** 11" (28 cm)

**Male:** Upland shorebird with 2 black bands around the neck, like a necklace. Brown back and white belly. Bright reddish-orange rump, visible in flight.

**Female:** same as male

**Juvenile:** similar to adults, with a single neck band

**Nest:** ground; male scrapes; 2 broods per year

**Eggs:** 3–5; tan with brown markings

**Incubation:** 24–28 days; male and female incubate

**Fledging:** 25 days; male and female lead their young to food

**Migration:** complete, to southern states, Mexico, Central America; non-migrator in southern half of Missouri

**Food:** insects, worms, snails

**Compare:** The Spotted Sandpiper (p. 139) is found around water but lacks the 2 neck bands of the Killdeer.

**Stan's Notes:** Technically classified as a shorebird but lives in dry habitats instead of the shore. Often found in vacant fields, gravel pits, driveways, wetland edges or along railroad tracks. The only shorebird that has two black neck bands. Known to fake a broken wing to draw intruders away from the nest; once the nest is safe, the parent will take flight. Nests are just a slight depression in a dry area and are often hard to see. Hatchlings look like miniature adults walking on stilts. Soon after hatching, the young follow their parents around and peck for insects. Gives a loud and distinctive "kill-deer" call. Migrates in small flocks.

# Brown Thrasher
*Toxostoma rufum*

**Size:** 11" (28 cm)

**Male:** Rust-red with a long tail. Heavy streaking on the breast and belly. Two white wing bars. Long, curved bill and bright-yellow eyes.

**Female:** same as male

**Juvenile:** same as adults but with grayish eyes

**Nest:** cup; female and male build; 2 broods per year

**Eggs:** 4–5; pale blue with brown markings

**Incubation:** 11–14 days; female and male incubate

**Fledging:** 10–13 days; female and male feed the young

**Migration:** complete, to southern states; non-migrator in southern Missouri

**Food:** insects, fruit

**Compare:** American Robin (p. 231) and Gray Catbird (p. 227) are similar but smaller and lack a streaked chest, rusty color and yellow eyes. Similar rusty color as Fox Sparrow (p. 119), but Brown Thrasher is larger and thinner. The Wood Thrush (p. 137) has a shorter brown tail and black eyes. Look for the long rusty-red tail to help identify the Brown Thrasher.

**Stan's Notes:** A prodigious songster. Sings along forest edges and in suburban yards. Often found in thick shrubs, where it will sing deliberate musical phrases, repeating each twice. The male Brown Thrasher has the largest documented repertoire of all North American songbirds, with more than 1,100 types of songs. Builds nest low in dense shrubs, often in fencerows. Quickly flies or runs on the ground in and out of thick shrubs. A noisy feeder due to its habit of turning over leaves, small rocks and branches to find food.

yellow-shafted
female

male

red-shafted
male

red-shafted
female

**YEAR-ROUND**

# Northern Flicker
*Colaptes auratus*

**Size:** 12" (30 cm)

**Male:** Brown and black with a black mustache and black necklace. Red spot on the nape of the neck. Speckled chest. Large white rump patch, seen only when flying.

**Female:** same as male but without a black mustache

**Juvenile:** same as adult of the same sex

**Nest:** cavity; female and male excavate; 1 brood per year

**Eggs:** 5–8; white without markings

**Incubation:** 11–14 days; female and male incubate

**Fledging:** 25–28 days; female and male feed the young

**Migration:** non-migrator in Missouri

**Food:** insects (especially ants and beetles); comes to suet feeders

**Compare:** The male Red-bellied Woodpecker (p. 57) has a red crown. Flickers are the only brown-backed woodpeckers in Missouri.

**Stan's Notes:** This is the only woodpecker to regularly feed on the ground. Prefers ants and beetles and produces an antacid saliva that neutralizes the acidic defense of ants. Can be attracted to your yard with a nest box stuffed with sawdust. Yellow-shafted variety has golden-yellow wing linings and tails. Male yellow-shafteds have black mustaches; male red-shafteds have red mustaches. Hybrids between varieties occur in the Great Plains, where ranges overlap. Often reuses an old nest. Undulates deeply during flight, flashing yellow under its wings and tail and calling "wacka-wacka" loudly. Populations swell in winter with northern migrants.

SUMMER

# Yellow-billed Cuckoo
*Coccyzus americanus*

**Size:** 12" (30 cm)

**Male:** Grayish brown head, back, wings and tail. White chin, chest and belly. Undertail distinctively patterned with bold black-and-white spots and lines. Long, downward-curved bill. Lower bill (mandible) is yellow.

**Female:** same as male

**Juvenile:** similar to adult, but undertail lacks bold black-and-white pattern, and bill lacks yellow

**Nest:** platform; female and male construct; 1–2 broods per year

**Eggs:** 2–6; light blue without markings

**Incubation:** 9–11 days; female and male incubate

**Fledging:** 7–9 days; female and male feed the young

**Migration:** complete, to South America

**Food:** insects

**Compare:** The large-sized, curved bill and bold black-and-white undertail markings make this bird hard to confuse with others.

**Stan's Notes:** Common summer resident throughout Missouri. Found in a wide variety of habitats, but usually nests along forest edges. Often will place a flimsy stick nest in a densely covered tree fork. Unlike many other birds, the young do not hatch at the same time (asynchronously). There can be many days between the first and last to hatch. A very short egg-to-fledging time with some young leaving the nest (fledging) after only one week. The first to fledge are attended by the male, while the female cares for the rest in the nest. Declining in population in many states.

# Mourning Dove
*Zenaida macroura*

**YEAR-ROUND**

| | |
|---|---|
| **Size:** | 12" (30 cm) |
| **Male:** | Smooth and fawn-colored. Gray patch on the head. Iridescent pink and greenish blue on the neck. Black spot behind and below the eyes. Black spots on the wings and tail. Pointed, wedged tail; white edges seen in flight. |
| **Female:** | similar to male, but lacks the pink-and-green iridescent neck feathers |
| **Juvenile:** | spotted and streaked plumage |
| **Nest:** | platform; female and male build; 2 broods per year |
| **Eggs:** | 2; white without markings |
| **Incubation:** | 13–14 days; male incubates during the day, female incubates at night |
| **Fledging:** | 12–14 days; female and male feed the young |
| **Migration:** | non-migrator to partial migrator; will move around to find food |
| **Food:** | seeds; will visit seed and ground feeders |
| **Compare:** | Eurasian Collared-Dove (p. 239) has a black collar on the nape of its neck. Smaller than Rock Pigeon (p. 241) and lacks its wide range of color combinations. |

**Stan's Notes:** Name comes from its mournful cooing. A ground feeder, bobbing its head as it walks. One of the few birds to drink without lifting its head, like the Rock Pigeon (p. 241). The parents feed the young (squab) a regurgitated liquid called crop-milk for their first few days of life. Platform nest is flimsy and often falls apart in storms. During takeoff and in flight, wind rushes through the bird's wing feathers, creating a characteristic whistling sound.

SUMMER
MIGRATION

# Upland Sandpiper
*Bartramia longicauda*

**Size:** 12" (30 cm)

**Male:** Overall brown shorebird. Long, yellow legs; a short, brown-tipped yellow bill; and white belly. Appears to have a thin neck and small head in relationship to its body.

**Female:** same as male

**Juvenile:** similar to adult

**Nest:** ground; female and male construct; 1 brood per year

**Eggs:** 3–4; off-white with red markings

**Incubation:** 21–27 days; female and male incubate

**Fledging:** 30–31 days; female and male feed young

**Migration:** complete, to South America

**Food:** insects, seeds

**Compare:** Breeding Spotted Sandpiper (p. 139) is smaller, has shorter legs, black spots on a white breast and is found in very different habitats. The Spotted Sandpiper is almost always near water while the Upland is in grassy meadows and prairies.

**Stan's Notes:** A shorebird of the dry grassland that is aptly named. Often seen standing on fence posts or other perches in a prairie or grassland habitat. Frequently found in prairies and grasslands that were burned, where foraging for food is easier. A true indicator of high-quality prairie habitat, this shorebird returns to a more watery habitat after breeding and just before migrating. Frequently holds its wings open over its back for several seconds just after landing. Formerly known as Upland Plover. Was hunted in the late 1800s.

winter

breeding

# Pied-billed Grebe
*Podilymbus podiceps*

**YEAR-ROUND**
SUMMER

**Size:** 12–14" (30–36 cm)

**Male:** Small and brown with a black chin and fluffy white patch beneath the tail. Black ring around a thick, chicken-like, ivory bill. Winter bill is brown and unmarked.

**Female:** same as male

**Juvenile:** paler than adults, with white spots and a gray chest, belly and bill

**Nest:** floating platform; female and male build; 1 brood per year

**Eggs:** 5–7; bluish white without markings

**Incubation:** 22–24 days; female and male incubate

**Fledging:** 45–60 days; female and male feed the young

**Migration:** complete, to southern states, Mexico and Central America

**Food:** crayfish, aquatic insects, fish

**Compare:** Look for a puffy white patch under the tail and thick, chicken-like bill to help identify.

**Stan's Notes:** A common resident waterbird, often seen diving for food. When disturbed, it slowly sinks like a submarine, quickly compressing its feathers, forcing the air out. Was called Hell-diver due to the length of time it can stay submerged. Able to surface far from where it went under. Well suited to life on water, with short wings, lobed toes, and legs set close to the rear of its body. Swims easily but moves awkwardly on land. Very sensitive to pollution. Builds nest on a floating mat in water. "Grebe" may originate from the Breton word *krib*, meaning "crest," referring to the crested head plumes of many grebes, especially during breeding season.

167

male
p. 39

female

YEAR-ROUND

# Great-tailed Grackle
*Quiscalus mexicanus*

| | |
|---|---|
| **Size:** | 15" (38 cm), female<br>18" (45 cm), male |
| **Female:** | An overall brown bird with a gray-to-brown belly. Light-brown-to-white eyes, eyebrows, throat and upper portion of chest. |
| **Male:** | all-black bird with iridescent purple sheen on head and back, exceptionally long tail, bright-yellow eyes |
| **Juvenile:** | similar to female |
| **Nest:** | cup; female builds; 1–2 broods per year |
| **Eggs:** | 3–5; greenish blue with brown markings |
| **Incubation:** | 12–14 days; female incubates |
| **Fledging:** | 21–23 days; female feeds young |
| **Migration:** | non-migrator to partial in Missouri; moves around to find food |
| **Food:** | insects, fruit, seeds; comes to seed feeders |
| **Compare:** | Female Brown-headed Cowbird (p. 131) is much smaller and lacks the female Grackle's lighter eyebrows. |

**Stan's Notes:** This is our largest grackle. It was once considered a subspecies of the Boat-tailed Grackle, which occurs along the Gulf Coast. Prefers to nest close to water in an open habitat. A colony nester. Males do not participate in nest building, incubation or raising young. Males rarely fight; females squabble over nest sites and materials. Several females mate with one male. The species is expanding northward, moving into northern states. Western populations tend to be larger than eastern. Song varies from population to population.

# Green-winged Teal
*Anas crecca*

**Size:** 14–15" (36–38 cm)

**Male:** Gray body. Chestnut head with a dark-green patch outlined with white from the eyes to the nape of the neck. Green patch on the wings (speculum), seen in flight. Butter-yellow tail.

**Female:** light brown with black spots and a green speculum; small bill

**Juvenile:** same as female

**Nest:** ground; female builds; 1 brood per year

**Eggs:** 8–10; creamy white without markings

**Incubation:** 21–23 days; female incubates

**Fledging:** 32–34 days; female teaches the young to feed

**Migration:** complete, to southern Missouri, southern states and Mexico

**Food:** aquatic plants and insects

**Compare:** The female Blue-winged Teal (p. 173) is similar in size, but it has slight white at the base of its bill. Look for the chestnut head with a dark-green patch on each side to identify the male Green-winged Teal.

**Stan's Notes:** One of the smallest dabbling ducks. Tips forward in water to feed off the bottom of shallow ponds. This behavior makes it vulnerable to ingesting spent lead shot, which can cause death. It walks well on land and will also feed in flooded fields and woodlands. Known for its fast and agile flight. Groups wheel and spin through the air in tight formation. The green wing patches are most obvious during flight.

male

female

SUMMER
MIGRATION

# Blue-winged Teal
*Spatula discors*

**Size:** 15–16" (38–41 cm)

**Male:** Small, plain-looking brown duck with black speckles and a large, crescent-shaped white mark at the base of the bill. Gray head. Black tail with a small white patch. Blue wing patch (speculum), best seen in flight.

**Female:** duller than male, with only slight white at the base of the bill; lacks a crescent mark on the face and a white patch on the tail

**Juvenile:** same as female

**Nest:** ground; female builds; 1 brood per year

**Eggs:** 8–11; creamy white

**Incubation:** 23–27 days; female incubates

**Fledging:** 35–44 days; female feeds the young

**Migration:** complete, to southern states, Mexico and Central America

**Food:** aquatic plants, seeds, aquatic insects

**Compare:** Female Green-winged Teal (p. 171) lacks white near its bill. The female Mallard (p. 185) has an orange-and-black bill. The female Wood Duck (p. 179) has a crest.

**Stan's Notes:** One of the few breeding ducks in Missouri and one of the longest-distance migrating ducks, with widespread nesting as far north as Alaska. An early migrator in the state, most leave before other, more northern ducks arrive in the fall. Constructs nest some distance from water. Female performs a distraction display to protect nest and young. Male leaves female near the end of incubation. Planting crops and cultivating to pond edges have caused a decline in population.

female

male p. 61

# Lesser Scaup
*Aythya affinis*

WINTER

**Size:** 16–17" (40–43 cm)

**Female:** Overall brown duck with a dull-white patch at the base of a light-gray bill. Yellow eyes.

**Male:** white and gray; the chest and head appear nearly black but the head looks purple with green highlights in direct sun; yellow eyes

**Juvenile:** same as female

**Nest:** ground; female builds; 1 brood per year

**Eggs:** 8–14; olive-buff without markings

**Incubation:** 22–28 days; female incubates

**Fledging:** 45–50 days; female teaches young to feed

**Migration:** complete, to southern states, Mexico, Central America and northern South America; winters in Missouri

**Food:** aquatic plants and insects

**Compare:** Male Blue-winged Teal (p. 173) is slightly smaller and has a crescent-shaped white mark at the base of bill. Female Wood Duck (p. 179) is larger with white around eyes. Look for the white patch at base of bill to help identify female Lesser Scaup.

**Stan's Notes:** A common wintering duck in Missouri. Often seen in large flocks on lakes and ponds. Submerges completely to feed on the bottom (unlike dabbling ducks, which only tip forward to reach the bottom). Note the bold white stripe under the wings when in flight. The male leaves the female when she starts incubating eggs. The quantity of eggs (clutch size) increases with the female's age. This species has an interesting babysitting arrangement in which groups of young (crèches) are tended by one to three adult females.

displaying

non-displaying

# Greater Prairie-Chicken

*Tympanuchus cupido*

YEAR-ROUND

**Size:** 17" (43 cm)

**Male:** A chicken-like brown bird. White barring throughout. Short, rounded tail, fans out for display. Orange-to-yellow patches (air sacs) on the sides of neck and bright orange-to-yellow eyebrows (combs) during display.

**Female:** similar to male, darker with a tan throat

**Juvenile:** similar to adults

**Nest:** ground; female builds; 1 brood per year

**Eggs:** 7–12; olive with brown markings

**Incubation:** 23–24 days; female incubates

**Fledging:** 7–10 days; female shows young what to eat

**Migration:** non-migrator; moves around to find food

**Food:** insects, seeds, fruit

**Compare:** Wild Turkey (p. 201) is much larger and darker and has a longer tail and neck. Northern Bobwhite (p. 151) is smaller, with a prominent white eye stripe and reddish-brown sides and belly.

**Stan's Notes:** Market hunting and intensive agricultural practices have nearly eliminated this bird from much of its historical range, but it's now recovering nicely. Missouri is also home to Lesser Prairie-Chickens, which are slightly smaller and grayer overall. Many males perform a loud animated dance together in spring in shorter grassy areas called leks. They bow forward, inflating air sacs, fanning tails, stomping feet, and giving a low moan (like air blowing across the top of an open bottle). Females watch for males who perform the best, fly into the arena to mate, then go off to build a nest and lay eggs.

male
p. 261

female

# Wood Duck
*Aix sponsa*

YEAR-ROUND
SUMMER

**Size:** 17–20" (43–51 cm)

**Female:** Small, brown dabbling duck. Bright-white eye-ring and a not-so-obvious crest. Blue patch on wings (speculum), often hidden.

**Male:** highly ornamented, with a mostly green head and crest patterned with black and white; rusty chest, white belly and red eyes

**Juvenile:** similar to female

**Nest:** cavity; female lines an old woodpecker cavity or a nest box in a tree; 1 brood per year

**Eggs:** 10–15; creamy white without markings

**Incubation:** 28–36 days; female incubates

**Fledging:** 56–68 days; female teaches the young to feed

**Migration:** complete, to southern states; non-migrator in southern Missouri

**Food:** aquatic insects, plants, seeds

**Compare:** The female Mallard (p. 185) and female Blue-winged Teal (p. 173) lack the eye-ring and crest. The female Northern Shoveler (p. 183) is larger and has a large spoon-shaped bill.

**Stan's Notes:** A common duck of quiet, shallow backwater ponds. Nearly went extinct around 1900 due to overhunting, but it's doing well now. Nests in a tree cavity or a nest box in a tree. Seen flying in forests or perching on high branches. Female takes off with a loud, squealing call and enters the nest cavity from full flight. Lays some eggs in a neighboring nest (egg dumping), resulting in more than 20 eggs in some clutches. Hatchlings stay in the nest for 24 hours, then jump from as high as 60 feet (18 m) to the ground or water to follow their mother. They never return to the nest.

male
p. 249

female

# Gadwall

*Mareca strepera*

WINTER

**Size:** 19" (48 cm)

**Female:** Mottled brown with a pronounced color change from dark-brown body to light-brown neck and head. Bright-white wing linings, seen in flight. Small white wing patch, seen when swimming. Gray bill with orange sides.

**Male:** plump gray duck with a brown head and distinctive black rump, white belly, bright-white wing linings, small white wing patch, chestnut-tinged wings, gray bill

**Juvenile:** similar to female

**Nest:** ground; female lines the nest with fine grass and down feathers plucked from her chest; 1 brood per year

**Eggs:** 8–11; white without markings

**Incubation:** 24–27 days; female incubates

**Fledging:** 48–56 days; young feed themselves

**Migration:** complete, to Missouri, southern states and Mexico

**Food:** aquatic insects

**Compare:** Female Mallard (p. 185) is similar but has a blue-and-white wing mark. Look for Gadwall's white wing patch and gray bill with orange sides.

**Stan's Notes:** A duck of shallow marshes. Consumes mostly plant material, dunking its head in water to feed rather than tipping forward, like other dabbling ducks. Walks well on land; feeds in fields and woodlands. Nests within 300 feet (90 m) of water. Often in pairs with other duck species. Establishes pair bond during winter.

male p. 265

female

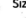

# Northern Shoveler
*Spatula clypeata*

**Size:** 19–21" (48–53 cm)

**Female:** A medium-sized brown duck speckled with black. Green patch on the wings (speculum). An extraordinarily large, spoon-shaped bill.

**Male:** iridescent green head, rusty sides, white chest and a large spoon-shaped bill

**Juvenile:** same as female

**Nest:** ground; female builds; 1 brood per year

**Eggs:** 9–12; olive without markings

**Incubation:** 22–25 days; female incubates

**Fledging:** 30–60 days; female leads the young to food

**Migration:** complete, to southern states, Mexico, Central America; winters in southern Missouri

**Food:** aquatic insects, plants

**Compare:** Female Mallard (p. 185) is similar but lacks the Shoveler's large bill. Female Wood Duck (p. 179) is smaller and has a white eye-ring. Look for Shoveler's large spoon-shaped bill to help identify.

**Stan's Notes:** One of several species of shovelers. Called "Shoveler" due to the peculiar, shovel-like shape of its bill. Given the common name "Northern" because it is the only species of these ducks in North America. Seen in shallow wetlands, ponds and small lakes in flocks of 5–10 birds. Flocks fly in tight formation. Swims low in water, pointing its large bill toward the water as if it's too heavy to lift. Usually swims in tight circles while feeding. Feeds mainly by filtering tiny aquatic insects and plants from the surface of the water with its bill.

male
p. 263

female

# Mallard
*Anas platyrhynchos*

YEAR-ROUND

**Size:** 19–21" (48–53 cm)

**Female:** Brown duck with a blue-and-white wing mark (speculum). Orange-and-black bill.

**Male:** large green head, white necklace, rust-brown or chestnut chest, combination of gray-and-white sides, yellow bill, orange legs and feet

**Juvenile:** same as female but with a yellow bill

**Nest:** ground; female builds; 1 brood per year

**Eggs:** 7–10; greenish to whitish, unmarked

**Incubation:** 26–30 days; female incubates

**Fledging:** 42–52 days; female leads the young to food

**Migration:** non-migrator to partial migrator in Missouri

**Food:** seeds, plants, aquatic insects; will come to ground feeders offering corn

**Compare:** Female Gadwall (p. 181) has a gray bill with orange sides. Female Northern Pintail (p. 187) is similar to female Mallard, but it has a gray bill. Female Northern Shoveler (p. 183) has a spoon-shaped bill. Female Wood Duck (p. 179) has a white eye-ring.

**Stan's Notes:** A familiar dabbling duck of lakes and ponds. Also found in rivers, streams and some backyards. Tips forward to feed on vegetation on the bottom of shallow water. The name "Mallard" comes from the Latin word *masculus,* meaning "male," referring to the male's habit of taking no part in raising the young. Female and male have white underwings and white tails, but only the male has black central tail feathers that curl upward. The female gives a classic quack. Returns to its birthplace each year.

male

female

WINTER

# Northern Pintail
*Anas acuta*

**Size:** 20" (52 cm), female
25" (63 cm), male

**Male:** A slender, elegant duck with a brown head, white neck and gray body. Gray bill. Extremely long and narrow black tail. Non-breeding has a pale brown head that lacks the clear demarcation between the brown head and white neck. Lacks long tail feathers.

**Female:** mottled brown body with a paler head and neck, long tail, gray bill

**Juvenile:** similar to female

**Nest:** ground; female builds; 1 brood per year

**Eggs:** 6–9; olive-green without markings

**Incubation:** 22–25 days; female incubates

**Fledging:** 36–50 days; female teaches young to feed

**Migration:** partial migrator, to southern states, Mexico; winters in Missouri

**Food:** aquatic plants and insects, seeds

**Compare:** The male Northern Pintail has a distinctive brown head and white neck and unique long tail feathers. Female Mallard (p. 185) is similar to female Pintail, but Mallard has an orange bill with black spots.

**Stan's Notes:** A common dabbling duck of marshes in the winter. About 90 percent of its diet is aquatic plants, except when females feed heavily on aquatic insects prior to nesting, presumably to gain extra nutrients for egg production. Male holds tail upright from the water's surface. No other North American duck has such a long tail.

male
p. 247

female

soaring

# Northern Harrier
*Circus hudsonius*

**YEAR-ROUND**
**WINTER**

**Size:** 18–22" (45–56 cm); up to 4' wingspan

**Female:** Slender, low-flying hawk with a dark-brown back and brown streaking on the chest and belly. Large white rump patch. Thin, black tail bands and black wing tips. Yellow eyes.

**Male:** silver-gray with a large white rump patch and white belly; black wing tips; yellow eyes; faint, thin bands across the tail

**Juvenile:** similar to female, with an orange breast

**Nest:** ground; female and male construct; 1 brood per year

**Eggs:** 4–8; bluish white without markings

**Incubation:** 31–32 days; female incubates

**Fledging:** 30–35 days; male and female feed the young

**Migration:** partial migrator, to southern states, Mexico and Central America; winters in Missouri

**Food:** mice, snakes, insects, small birds

**Compare:** Slimmer than the Red-tailed Hawk (p. 191). Look for the characteristic low gliding and the black tail bands to identify the female Harrier.

**Stan's Notes:** One of the easiest of hawks to identify. Glides just above the ground, following the contours of the land while searching for prey. Holds its wings just above horizontal, tilting back and forth in the wind, similar to the Turkey Vulture. Formerly called Marsh Hawk due to its habit of hunting over marshes. Feeds and nests on the ground. Will also preen and rest on the ground. Unlike other hawks, mainly uses its hearing to find prey, followed by its sight. At any age, it has a distinctive owl-like face disk.

soaring

juvenile
soaring

juvenile

# Red-tailed Hawk

*Buteo jamaicensis*

YEAR-ROUND

**Size:** 19–23" (48–63 cm); up to 4½' wingspan

**Male:** Variety of colorations, from chocolate brown to nearly all white. Often brown with a white breast and brown belly band. Rust-red tail. Underside of wing is white with a small dark patch on the leading edge near the shoulder.

**Female:** same as male but slightly larger

**Juvenile:** similar to adults, with a speckled breast and light eyes; lacks a red tail

**Nest:** platform; male and female build; 1 brood per year

**Eggs:** 2–3; white without markings or sometimes marked with brown

**Incubation:** 30–35 days; female and male incubate

**Fledging:** 45–46 days; male and female feed the young

**Migration:** non-migrator to partial migrator

**Food:** small and medium-sized animals, large birds, snakes, fish, insects, bats, carrion

**Compare:** Cooper's Hawk (p. 243) and Sharp-shinned Hawk (p. 235) are much smaller and lack the red tail.

**Stan's Notes:** Common in open country and cities. Seen perching on fences, freeway lampposts and trees. Look for it circling above open fields and roadsides, searching for prey. Gives a high-pitched scream that trails off. Often builds a large stick nest in large trees along roads. Lines nest with finer material, like evergreen needles. Returns to the same nest site each year. The red tail develops in the second year and is best seen from above.

# Barred Owl
*Strix varia*

**YEAR-ROUND**

**Size:** 20–24" (51–61 cm); up to 3½' wingspan

**Male:** Chunky brown-and-gray owl. Dark horizontal barring on upper chest. Vertical streaks on lower chest and belly. A large head and dark-brown eyes. Yellow bill and feet.

**Female:** same as male but slightly larger

**Juvenile:** light gray with a black face

**Nest:** cavity; does not add any nesting material; 1 brood per year

**Eggs:** 2–3; white without markings

**Incubation:** 28–33 days; female incubates

**Fledging:** 42–44 days; female and male feed the young

**Migration:** non-migrator

**Food:** mice, rabbits and other animals, small birds, fish, reptiles; amphibians

**Compare:** Great Horned Owl (p. 195) has "horns," and the much smaller Eastern Screech-Owl (p. 225) has "ears," both of which the Barred Owl lacks. Look for a stocky owl with a large head and dark-brown eyes to identify the Barred Owl.

**Stan's Notes:** Prefers deciduous woodlands but can be attracted to your yard with a simple nest box that has a large entrance hole. Often seen hunting during the day. Perches and watches for mice, birds and other prey. Hovers over water and reaches down to grab fish. After fledging, the young stay with the parents for up to four months. Often sounds like a dog barking before calling six to eight hoots, sounding like "who-who-who-cooks-for-you."

YEAR-ROUND

# Great Horned Owl
*Bubo virginianus*

**Size:** 21–25" (53–64 cm); up to 4' wingspan

**Male:** Robust brown "horned" owl. Bright-yellow eyes and a V-shaped white throat resembling a necklace. Horizontal barring on the chest.

**Female:** same as male but slightly larger

**Juvenile:** similar to adults but lacks ear tufts

**Nest:** no nest; takes over the nest of a crow, hawk or Great Blue Heron or uses a partial cavity, stump or broken tree; 1 brood per year

**Eggs:** 2–3; white without markings

**Incubation:** 26–30 days; female incubates

**Fledging:** 30–35 days; male and female feed the young

**Migration:** non-migrator

**Food:** mammals, birds (ducks), snakes, insects

**Compare:** Barred Owl (p. 193) has dark eyes and no "horns." The Eastern Screech-Owl (p. 225) is extremely tiny. Look for bright-yellow eyes and feather "horns" on the head to help identify the Great Horned Owl.

**Stan's Notes:** One of the earliest nesting birds in the state, laying eggs in January and February. Able to hunt in complete darkness due to its excellent hearing. The "horns," or "ears," are tufts of feathers and have nothing to do with hearing. Cannot turn its head all the way around. Wing feathers are ragged on the ends, resulting in silent flight. Eyelids close from the top down, like humans. Fearless, it is one of the few animals that will kill skunks and porcupines. Given that, it is also called the Flying Tiger. Call sounds like "hoo-hoo-hoo-hoooo."

winter

breeding

in flight

# White-faced Ibis
*Plegadis chihi*

SUMMER
MIGRATION

**Size:** 23" (58 cm); up to 3' wingspan

**Male:** Appears brown with rusty red (chestnut) on upper body. Glossy brown with green sheen on lower body. Long, down-curved gray bill. White border on a light-red face. Orange-red legs and feet. Deep-red eyes. Winter has a gray mask and less chestnut.

**Female:** same as male

**Juvenile:** similar to winter adult

**Nest:** platform, on ground, low in shrub or small tree; female and male build; 1 brood a year

**Eggs:** 2–4; blue or green with brown markings

**Incubation:** 21–23 days; female and male incubate

**Fledging:** 30–35 days; female and male feed young

**Migration:** complete, to coastal U.S. and Mexico

**Food:** insects, crayfish, frogs, small fish, shellfish

**Compare:** Great Blue Heron (p. 253) is much larger. Look for the down-curved bill and dark body to identify the White-faced Ibis.

**Stan's Notes:** Of the three ibis species in the U.S., seen during migration. Usually found in marshes and estuaries. When near and in good light, appears glossy red with green, blue and purple highlights. Uses its long bill to find and eat aquatic insects and fish. Large groups fly in a straight line. Rapid, shallow wingbeats, then a short glide. Nests close to the water in large colonies with egrets and herons. Builds a loose nest of thin twigs, leaves and roots, lined with green leaves. Common name comes from the white outline on face.

male

female

# Ring-necked Pheasant
*Phasianus colchicus*

**YEAR-ROUND**

**Size:** 30–36" (76–91 cm), male, including tail
21–25" (53–64 cm), female, including tail

**Male:** Golden-brown body with a long tail. White ring around the neck. Head is purple, green, blue and red.

**Female:** smaller and less flamboyant than the male, with brown plumage and a long tail

**Juvenile:** similar to female, with a shorter tail

**Nest:** ground; female builds; 1 brood per year

**Eggs:** 8–10; olive-brown without markings

**Incubation:** 23–25 days; female incubates

**Fledging:** 11–12 days; female leads the young to food

**Migration:** non-migrator

**Food:** insects, seeds, fruit; visits ground feeders

**Compare:** The Ring-necked Pheasant has a long tail, and the male is brightly colored.

**Stan's Notes:** Originally introduced to North America from China in the late 1800s. Introduction in Missouri started in 1904 but was unsuccessful. A successful second attempt started in the 1920–30s and continues today. Widespread in northern Missouri. Like many other game birds, its numbers vary greatly, making it common in some years, scarce in others. Seeks shelter during harsh winter weather. To attract females, the male gives a cackling call and then rapidly flutters his wings. Takes off in an explosive flight with fast wingbeats followed by gliding low to the ground. The name "Ring-necked" refers to the white ring around the male's neck. "Pheasant" comes from the Greek word *phaisianos*, which means "bird of the River Phasis" (known today as the Rioni River).

displaying male

non-displaying

female

# Wild Turkey
*Meleagris gallopavo*

YEAR-ROUND

**Size:** 36–48" (91–122 cm)

**Male:** Large brown-and-bronze bird with a na_ blue-and-red head. Long, straight, black _ in the center of the chest. Tail spreads ope_ like a fan. Spurs on legs.

**Female:** thinner and less striking than the male; often lacks a breast beard

**Juvenile:** same as adult of the same sex

**Nest:** ground; female builds; 1 brood per year

**Eggs:** 10–12; buff-white with dull-brown markings

**Incubation:** 27–28 days; female incubates

**Fledging:** 6–10 days; female leads the young to food

**Migration:** non-migrator; moves around to find food

**Food:** insects, seeds, fruit

**Compare:** This bird is quite distinctive and unlikely to be confused with others.

**Stan's Notes:** The largest game bird in Missouri, and the species from which the domestic turkey was bred. A strong flier that can approach 60 miles (97 km) per hour. Can fly straight up, then away. Eyesight is three times better than ours. Hearing is also excellent; can hear competing males up to a mile away. Male has a "harem" of up to 20 females. Female scrapes out a shallow depression for nesting and pads it with soft leaves. Males are known as toms, females are hens, and young are poults. Roosts in trees at night. Eliminated from many of the eastern states by the turn of the 20th century due to market hunting and loss of habitat, and reintroduced in the 1960–80s. Populations are now stable.

# Ruby-crowned Kinglet
*Regulus calendula*

MIGRATION
WINTER

| | |
|---|---|
| **Size:** | 4" (10 cm) |
| **Male:** | Small, teardrop-shaped green-to-gray bird. Two white wing bars and a white eye-ring. Hidden ruby crown. |
| **Female:** | same as male, but lacks a ruby crown |
| **Juvenile:** | same as female |
| **Nest:** | pendulous; female builds; 1 brood per year |
| **Eggs:** | 4–5; white with brown markings |
| **Incubation:** | 11–12 days; female incubates |
| **Fledging:** | 11–12 days; female and male feed the young |
| **Migration:** | complete, to southern states, Mexico, Central America; winters in southeastern Missouri |
| **Food:** | insects, berries |
| **Compare:** | The female American Goldfinch (p. 301) shares the drab olive plumage and unmarked chest, but it is larger. Look for the white eye-ring to identify the Ruby-crowned Kinglet. |

**Stan's Notes:** This is one of the smaller birds in the state. Most commonly seen during the spring and autumn migrations. Look for it flitting around thick shrubs low to the ground. It takes a quick eye to see the ruby crown, which the male flashes when he is excited. The female weaves an unusually intricate nest and fastens colorful lichens and mosses to the exterior with spiderwebs. Often builds the nest high in a mature tree, where it hangs from a branch that has overlapping leaves. Sings a distinctive song that starts out soft and ends loud and on a higher note. "Kinglet" originates from the word *king*, referring to the male's red crown, and the diminutive suffix *let*, meaning "small."

# Red-breasted Nuthatch

*Sitta canadensis*

WINTER

**Size:** 4½" (11 cm)

**Male:** Gray-backed bird with an obvious bla[ck] line and black cap. Rust-red breast an[d]

**Female:** duller than male and has a gray cap and pale undersides

**Juvenile:** same as female

**Nest:** cavity; male and female excavate a cavity or move into a vacant hole; 1 brood per year

**Eggs:** 5–6; white with red-brown markings

**Incubation:** 11–12 days; female incubates

**Fledging:** 14–20 days; female and male feed the young

**Migration:** irruptive; moves around Missouri in search of food

**Food:** insects, insect eggs, seeds; comes to seed and suet feeders

**Compare:** The White-breasted Nuthatch (p. 211) is larger and has a white breast. Look for the rust-red breast and black eye line to help identify the Red-breasted Nuthatch.

**Stan's Notes:** The nuthatch climbs down trunks of trees headfirst, searching for insects. Like a chickadee, it grabs a seed from a feeder and flies off to crack it open. It wedges the seed into a crevice and pounds it open with several sharp blows. The name "Nuthatch" comes from the Middle English moniker *nuthak,* referring to the habit of hacking seeds open. Look for it in mature conifers, where it extracts seeds from pine cones. Excavates a cavity or takes an old woodpecker hole or a natural cavity and builds a nest within. An irruptive migrator, common in some winters and scarce in others. Gives a series of nasal "yank-yank-yank" calls.

# Black-capped Chickadee
*Poecile atricapillus*

**Size:** 5" (13 cm)

**Male:** Familiar gray bird with a black cap and th[r...] patch. Tan sides and belly. White chest. Sm[...] white wing marks.

**Female:** same as male

**Juvenile:** same as adult

**Nest:** cavity; female and male excavate or use a nest box; 1 brood per year

**Eggs:** 5–7; white with fine brown markings

**Incubation:** 11–13 days; female and male incubate

**Fledging:** 14–18 days; female and male feed the young

**Migration:** non-migrator

**Food:** insects, seeds, fruit; comes to seed and suet feeders

**Compare:** Identical to Carolina Chickadee (p. 209), except in song. Carolina's song is a higher, faster version of Black-capped Chickadee's. Tufted Titmouse (p. 217) is larger than the Black-capped Chickadee and has a crest.

**Stan's Notes:** A widespread and common bird throughout the northern half of Missouri. Backyard bird that can be attracted with a nest box or bird feeder. Can be easily tamed and hand-fed. Much of the diet comes from bird feeders, so it can be a common urban bird. Needs to feed every day in winter, and forages to find food even during the worst winter storms. Typically seen with nuthatches, woodpeckers and other birds. Builds nest mostly with green moss and lines it with fur. Named "Chickadee" for its familiar "chika-dee-dee-dee-dee" call. Also gives a high-pitched, two-toned "fee-bee" call. Can have different calls in different regions.

# Carolina Chickadee
*Poecile caroline...*

**Size:** 5" (13 cm)

**Male:** Mostly gray with a black cap an...
White face and chest with a tan b...
Darker-gray tail.

**Female:** same as male

**Juvenile:** same as adult

**Nest:** cavity; female and male build or excavate;
1–2 broods per year

**Eggs:** 5–7; white with reddish-brown markings

**Incubation:** 11–12 days; female and male incubate

**Fledging:** 13–17 days; female and male feed the young

**Migration:** non-migrator

**Food:** insects, seeds, fruit; comes to seed and
suet feeders

**Compare:** Identical to Black-capped Chickadee (p. 207),
except in song. Carolina's song is a higher,
faster version of Black-capped Chickadee's.
Tufted Titmouse (p. 217) is a close relative,
but it has an erect crest and lacks the black
cap and chin.

**Stan's Notes:** A common bird in Missouri. One of the first birds to use a newly placed feeder. Flies to a feeder, grabs a seed and carries it to a branch. To get to the meat inside, it holds the seed down with its feet and hammers the shell open with its bill. Returns for another seed. A friendly bird. Can be tamed and hand-fed. Attracted with a nest box that has a 1¼-inch entrance hole. Female gives a loud snake-like hiss if disturbed on the nest. Often seen with other birds (mixed flock) in winter. Song is a high, fast "chika-dee-dee-dee-dee."

male

female

# White-brea...

*Sitta caro...*

**Size:** 5–6" (13–15 cm)

**Male:** Slate gray with a white face, ... nape. Bill is long and thin, slightly Chestnut undertail.

**Female:** similar to male, but has a gray cap and ...

**Juvenile:** similar to female

**Nest:** cavity; female and male build a nest within; 1 brood per year

**Eggs:** 5–7; white with brown markings

**Incubation:** 11–12 days; female incubates

**Fledging:** 13–14 days; female and male feed the young

**Migration:** non-migrator

**Food:** insects, insect eggs, seeds; comes to seed and suet feeders

**Compare:** Red-breasted Nuthatch (p. 205) is smaller and has a rust-red belly and distinctive black eye line. Look for the white breast to help identify the White-breasted Nuthatch.

**Stan's Notes:** The nuthatch hops headfirst down trees, looking for insects missed by birds climbing up. Its climbing agility is due to an extra-long hind toe claw, or nail, that is nearly twice the size of its front claws. "Nuthatch," from the Middle English *nuthak*, refers to the bird's habit of wedging a seed in a crevice and hacking it open. Often seen in flocks with chickadees and Downy Woodpeckers. A year-round resident that is abundant throughout Missouri. Mates stay together year-round, defending a small territory. Gives a characteristic "whi-whi-whi-whi" spring call during February and March. One of nearly 30 worldwide nuthatch species.

211

male

female

first winter

# Yellow-ru...

*Setopha...*

**Size:** 5–6" (13–15 cm)

**Male:** Slate gray with black streak... Yellow patches on the head, t... White chin and belly. Two white ...

**Female:** duller gray than the male, mixed wit...

**Juvenile:** first winter is similar to the adult female

**Nest:** cup; female builds; 2 broods per year

**Eggs:** 4–5; white with brown markings

**Incubation:** 12–13 days; female incubates

**Fledging:** 10–12 days; female and male feed young

**Migration:** complete, to southern states, Mexico and Central America; winters in Missouri

**Food:** insects, berries; visits suet feeders in spring

**Compare:** The male Common Yellowthroat (p. 303) has a yellow chest and distinctive black mask. The male Yellow Warbler (p. 305) is all yellow with orange streaks on breast. Look for patches of yellow on the rump, head, flanks and chin of Yellow-rumped Warbler to help identify.

**Stan's Notes:** Common wintering warbler in Missouri, one of the few to spend the winter. Flocks of hundreds seen during migration. Usually arrives the last week of September or first week of October. By November very few are found in northern Missouri. Males molt to a dull color each winter similar to females, retaining the yellow patches. Sometimes called Butter-butts due to the yellow patch on rump. Formerly called Audubon's Warbler. Familiar call is a robust "chip." Nests in conifer and aspen forests, but not in Missouri.

female p. 97

male

# Dark-
*Junco*

**Size:** 5½" (14 cm)

**Male:** Plump, dark-eyed bird with charcoal chest, head and back. Pink bill. White outer tail feathers like a white V in flight.

**Female:** round with brown plumage

**Juvenile:** similar to female, with streaking on the bre_ and head

**Nest:** cup; female and male build; 2 broods per year

**Eggs:** 3–5; white with reddish-brown markings

**Incubation:** 12–13 days; female incubates

**Fledging:** 10–13 days; male and female feed the young

**Migration:** complete, throughout the U.S.; winters in Missouri

**Food:** seeds, insects; visits ground and seed feeders

**Compare:** Rarely confused with any other bird. Look for the pink bill and small flocks feeding under feeders to identify the male Dark-eyed Junco.

**Stan's Notes:** One of the most common birds in the state during winter. Nests in a wide variety of wooded habitats. Adheres to a rigid social hierarchy, with dominant birds chasing the less dominant ones. Look for the white outer tail feathers flashing in flight. Often seen in small flocks on the ground, where it uses its feet to simultaneously "double-scratch" to expose seeds and insects. Eats many weed seeds. Several junco species have now been combined into one, simply called Dark-eyed Junco. Males don't go as far south as females in winter. Doesn't nest in Missouri.

## Tufte...
*Baeolop...*

**Size:** 6" (15 cm)

**Male:** Slate gray with a white che... Pointed crest. Rust-brown wa... flanks. Gray legs and dark eyes.

**Female:** same as male

**Juvenile:** same as adult

**Nest:** cavity; female lines an old woodpecker cavity; 2 broods per year

**Eggs:** 5-7; white with brown markings

**Incubation:** 13-14 days; female incubates

**Fledging:** 15-18 days; female and male feed the young

**Migration:** non-migrator

**Food:** insects, seeds, fruit; will come to seed and suet feeders

**Compare:** Closely related to the slightly smaller Black-capped Chickadee (p. 207) and Carolina Chickadee (p. 209). Chickadees lack the crest of Titmouse. Similar in size and color to the White-breasted Nuthatch (p. 211), but Nuthatch doesn't have a crest.

**Stan's Notes:** A common feeder bird that can be attracted with an offering of black oil sunflower seeds or suet. Well known for its "peter-peter-peter" call, which it quickly repeats. Notorious for pulling hair from sleeping dogs, cats and squirrels to line its nest. Usually seen only one or two at a time. The prefix *tit* in the common name comes from a Scandinavian word meaning "little." Suffix *mouse* is derived from the Old English word *mase*, meaning "bird." Simply translated, it is a "small bird."

217

## Eastern...

*Sayornis...*

**Size:** 6½" (18 cm)

**Male:** Plain gray with slightly darke_ a light-olive belly and a thin, da

**Female:** same as male

**Juvenile:** same as adults

**Nest:** cup; female builds; 2 broods per year

**Eggs:** 4–5; white without markings

**Incubation:** 15–16 days; female incubates

**Fledging:** 15–16 days; male and female feed the young

**Migration:** complete, to southern states and Mexico

**Food:** insects

**Compare:** The Gray Catbird (p. 227) has a black crown and a chestnut patch under its tail. Eastern Phoebe lacks any distinctive markings. Listen for its well-enunciated "fee-bee" call and look for the hawking and tail-pumping behaviors to help identify this bird.

**Stan's Notes:** A sparrow-size bird that often perches on the end of a dead branch. Found in forests, yards and farms. In a process called hawking, it waits for a passing insect. When a bug flies near, it launches out to catch it and then returns to the same branch. It has a distinctive habit of pumping its tail up and down while perching. Builds nest beneath the eaves of houses, under bridges or in other sheltered spots. Uses mud, grass and moss for nest materials and hair (and sometimes feathers) for the lining. The common name is derived from its distinctive "fee-bee" call, which it repeats over and over from the tops of dead branches.

219

# Great Cre...

*Myiarchu...*

SUMMER

**Size:** 8" (20 cm)

**Male:** Gray head with a prominen... and throat. Yellow from the be... of a reddish-brown tail. Lower b...
the base.

**Female:** same as male

**Juvenile:** same as adults

**Nest:** cavity; female and male constru...t; 1 brood per year

**Eggs:** 4–6; white or buff with brown markings

**Incubation:** 13–15 days; female inc...ates

**Fledging:** 14–21 days; female and male feed the young

**Migration:** complete, to Mexico and Central America

**Food:** insects, fruit

**Compare:** The Eastern Kingbird (p. 223) has a white band across its tail. The Eastern Phoebe (p. 219) is simila..., but it lacks a crest and yellow belly. Look for the crest to identify the Flycatcher.

**Stan's Notes:** Higher concentrations are in southern Missouri, but breeds throughou... the state. It lives high up in trees, rarely coming to the ground. Makes long flights from treetop to treetop, moving from one hunting area to another. Gleans insects from tree leaves. Often hear... before seen. "Great Crested" refers to the set of extra-long feathers on top of its head (crest), which the bird raises when alert or agitated, like the Northern Cardinal. Nests in an old woodpecker hole but can be attracted with a man-made nest box that has an entrance hole 1½–2½ inches (4–6 cm) in diameter. Often stuffs the cavity with a collection of fur, feathers, string and snake skins.

# Eastern

*Tyrannus ty...*

**Size:** 8" (20 cm)

**Male:** Mostly gray and black with a belly. Black head and tail with a band on the tip of the tail. Concea... crown, rarely seen.

**Female:** same as male

**Juvenile:** same as adults

**Nest:** cup; male and female build; 1 brood per year

**Eggs:** 3–4; white with brown markings

**Incubation:** 16–18 days; female incubates

**Fledging:** 16–18 days; female and male feed the young

**Migration:** complete, to Mexico, Central America and South America

**Food:** insects, fruit

**Compare:** American Robin (p. 231) is larger and has a rust-red breast. The Eastern Phoebe (p. 219) is smaller and has an olive-green belly.

**Stan's Notes:** A common bird throughout Missouri in open fields and prairies. Autumn migration begins in late August and early September, with groups of up to 20 individuals migrating together. Returns to the mating ground in spring, where pairs defend their territory. Seems to be unafraid of other birds and chases larger birds. Given the common name "King" for its bold attitude and behavior. In a hunting technique known as hawking, it perches on a branch and watches for insects, flies out to catch one, and then returns to the same perch. Swoops from perch to perch when hunting. Becomes very vocal during late summer, when family members call back and forth to one another while hunting for insects.

red morph

gray morph

# Eastern Screech-Owl

*Megascops asio*

**YEAR-ROUND**

**Size:** 8–10" (20–25 cm); up to 2' wingspan

**Male:** Small "eared" owl that occurs in different colorations. Gray morph is mottled gray and white. Red morph is mottled rust and white. Short wings. Bright-yellow eyes.

**Female:** same as male but slightly larger

**Juvenile:** lighter color than adults of the same morph and usually lacks ear tufts

**Nest:** cavity, old woodpecker cavity, or man-made nest box; does not add any nesting material; 1 brood per year

**Eggs:** 4–5; white without markings

**Incubation:** 25–26 days; female incubates, male feeds the female during incubation

**Fledging:** 26–27 days; male and female feed the young

**Migration:** non-migrator; moves around in winter

**Food:** large insects, small mammals, birds, snakes

**Compare:** Eastern Screech-Owl is hard to confuse with its considerably larger cousin, the Great Horned Owl (p. 195).

**Stan's Notes:** Commonly found in areas that have suitable natural cavities for nesting and roosting. Active from dusk to dawn. Usually gives a tremulous, descending trill, like a sound effect in a scary movie. Seldom gives a screeching call. Often seen sunning itself at a nest-box hole during winter. Mates may have a long-term pair bond and may roost together at night. Excellent hearing and eyesight. Flaps rapidly and flies silently. Has winter and summer territories. The gray morph is more common than the red.

SUMMER

# Gray Catbird
*Dumetella carolinensis*

**Size:** 9" (22.5 cm)

**Male:** Handsome slate-gray bird with a black crown and a long, thin, black bill. Often lifts up its tail, exposing a chestnut patch beneath.

**Female:** same as male

**Juvenile:** same as adults

**Nest:** cup; female and male build; 2 broods per year

**Eggs:** 4–6; blue-green without markings

**Incubation:** 12–13 days; female incubates

**Fledging:** 10–11 days; female and male feed young

**Migration:** complete, to southern states

**Food:** insects, occasional fruit; visits suet feeders

**Compare:** The Eastern Phoebe (p. 219) is smaller and has an olive belly. The Eastern Kingbird (p. 223) is similar in size but has a white belly and a white band across its tail. To identify the Gray Catbird, look for the black crown and chestnut patch under the tail.

**Stan's Notes:** Returns to Missouri by the last week of April. Seen in great numbers during the autumn migration in the last week of September and early October. A secretive bird, more often heard than seen. The Chippewa Indians gave it a name that means "the bird that cries with grief" due to its raspy call. Called "Catbird" because the sound is like the meowing of a house cat. Often mimics other birds, rarely repeating the same phrases. More frequently heard than seen. Nests in thick shrubs and quickly flies back into shrubs if approached. If a cowbird lays an egg in its nest, the catbird will quickly break it and eject it.

YEAR-ROUND

# Loggerhead Shrike
*Lanius ludovicianus*

**Size:** 9" (22.5 cm)

**Male:** Gray head and back. Black wings, tail, legs and feet. White chin, breast and belly. Black mask across the eyes. Black bill with a hooked tip. White wing patches, seen in flight.

**Female:** same as male

**Juvenile:** dull version of adult

**Nest:** cup; male and female construct; 1–2 broods per year

**Eggs:** 4–7; off-white with dark markings

**Incubation:** 16–17 days; female incubates

**Fledging:** 17–21 days; female and male feed the young

**Migration:** complete to partial-migrator; non-migrator in Missouri

**Food:** insects, lizards, small mammals, frogs

**Compare:** The Northern Mockingbird (p. 233) has a similar color pattern, but it lacks the black mask. The Cedar Waxwing (p. 133) has a black mask, but it is a brown bird, not gray and black like the Loggerhead Shrike.

**Stan's Notes:** The Loggerhead is a songbird that acts like a bird of prey. Known for skewering prey on barbed wire fences, thorns and other sharp objects to store or hold still while tearing apart to eat, hence its other common name, Butcher Bird. Feet are too weak to hold the prey it eats. Common throughout Missouri. Will migrate, but rarely is noticed due to the relatively large non-migrating winter population. Breeding bird surveys indicate declining populations in the Great Plains due to pesticides killing its major food source—grasshoppers. It is abundant, however, in the Show-Me State.

# American Robin
*Turdus migratorius*

YEAR-ROUND

**Size:** 9–11" (23–28 cm)

**Male:** Familiar gray bird with a dark rust-red breast and a nearly black head and tail. White chin with black streaks. White eye-ring.

**Female:** similar to male, with a duller rust-red breast and a gray head

**Juvenile:** similar to female, with a speckled breast and brown back

**Nest:** cup; female builds with help from the male; 2–3 broods per year

**Eggs:** 4–7; pale blue without markings

**Incubation:** 12–14 days; female incubates

**Fledging:** 14–16 days; female and male feed the young

**Migration:** complete, to southern states, Mexico, Central America; non-migrator in Missouri

**Food:** insects, fruit, berries, earthworms

**Compare:** Familiar bird to all. To differentiate the male from the female, compare the nearly black head and rust-red chest of the male with the gray head and duller chest of the female.

**Stan's Notes:** Although complete migrators in northern states, the robin is a year-round resident in Missouri. Can be heard singing all night long during spring. City robins sing louder than country robins in order to hear one another over traffic and noise. A robin isn't listening for worms when it turns its head to one side. It is focusing its sight out of one eye to look for dirt moving, which is caused by worms moving. Territorial, often fighting its reflection in a window.

displaying

**YEAR-ROUND**

# Northern Mockingbird
*Mimus polyglottos*

**Size:** 10" (25 cm)

**Male:** Silvery-gray head and back with a light-gray breast and belly. White wing patches, seen in flight or during display. Tail mostly black with white outer tail feathers. Black bill.

**Female:** same as male

**Juvenile:** dull gray with a heavily streaked breast and a gray bill

**Nest:** cup; female and male construct; 2 broods per year, sometimes more

**Eggs:** 3–5; blue-green with brown markings

**Incubation:** 12–13 days; female incubates

**Fledging:** 11–13 days; female and male feed the young

**Migration:** partial, to southern states; non-migrator in most of Missouri

**Food:** insects, fruit

**Compare:** Loggerhead Shrike (p. 229) has a similar color pattern, but it is stockier, has a black mask and perches in more-open places. The Gray Catbird (p. 227) is slate gray and lacks wing patches.

**Stan's Notes:** A very animated bird. Performs an elaborate mating dance. Facing each other with heads and tails erect, pairs will run toward each other, flashing their white wing patches, and then retreat to cover nearby. Thought to flash the wing patches to scare up insects when hunting. Sits for long periods on top of shrubs. Imitates other birds (vocal mimicry); hence the common name. Young males often sing at night. Often unafraid of people, allowing for close observation.

soaring

juvenile

# Sharp-shinned Hawk

*Accipiter striatus*

YEAR-ROUND
WINTER

**Size:** 10–14" (25–36 cm); up to 2' wingspan

**Male:** Small woodland hawk with a gray back and head and a rust-red chest. Short wings. Long, squared tail and several dark tail bands, with the widest at the end of the tail. Red eyes.

**Female:** same as male but larger

**Juvenile:** same size as adults, with a brown back, heavy streaking on the chest and yellow eyes

**Nest:** platform; female builds; 1 brood per year

**Eggs:** 4–5; white with brown markings

**Incubation:** 32–35 days; female incubates

**Fledging:** 24–27 days; female and male feed the young

**Migration:** complete, to southern states, Mexico and Central America; winters in Missouri

**Food:** birds, small mammals

**Compare:** Cooper's Hawk (p. 243) is larger and has a larger head, a slightly longer neck and a rounded tail. Look for the squared tail to help identify the Sharp-shinned Hawk.

**Stan's Notes:** A hawk of backyards, parks and woodlands. Seen swooping on birds visiting feeders and chasing them as they flee. Its short wingspan and long tail help it to maneuver through thick stands of trees in pursuit of prey. Calls a loud, high-pitched "kik-kik-kik-kik." Named "Sharp-shinned" for the sharp projection (keel) on the leading edge of its shin. A bird's shin is actually below the ankle (rather than above it, like ours) on the tarsus bone of its foot. In most birds, the tarsus bone is rounded, not sharp.

soaring

juvenile

soaring
juvenile

# Mississippi Kite
*Ictinia mississippiensis*

SUMMER
MIGRATION

**Size:** 12–15" (30–38 cm); up to 2¾' wingspan

**Male:** Overall gray bird with a paler, nearly white head. Nearly black tail. Dark eye patch surrounding red eyes. Short, hooked gray bill. Yellow legs and feet.

**Female:** same as male

**Juvenile:** similar to adult but has a brown chest with vertical white streaks

**Nest:** platform; female and male build; 1 brood per year

**Eggs:** 1–2; white without markings

**Incubation:** 29–32 days; female and male incubate

**Fledging:** 32–34 days; female and male feed young

**Migration:** complete, to South America

**Food:** insects, lizards, small snakes

**Compare:** Smaller than many other birds of prey. The overall gray appearance with a lighter head makes it easy to identify.

**Stan's Notes:** A bird of prey that eats mostly large insects. Groups follow livestock, feeding on insects they kick up. Hunts insects by soaring or hovering, catching in flight or diving down. It requires open areas with scattered trees for nesting. Nests in semi-colonies. Mated pairs aggressively defend nest sites. Individuals often stray out of traditional ranges, appearing in northern states and up the East Coast.

# Eurasian Collared-Dove
*Streptopelia decaocto*

YEAR-ROUND

**Size:** 12½" (32 cm)

**Male:** Head, neck, breast and belly are gray to tan. Back, wings and tail are slightly darker. Thin, black collar with a white border on the nape of the neck. Tail is long and squared.

**Female:** same as male

**Juvenile:** similar to adults

**Nest:** platform; female and male build; 2–3 broods per year

**Eggs:** 3–5; creamy white without markings

**Incubation:** 12–14 days; female and male incubate

**Fledging:** 12–14 days; female and male feed the young

**Migration:** non-migrator, moves around to find food

**Food:** seeds; will visit ground and seed feeders

**Compare:** The Mourning Dove (p. 163) is slightly smaller and darker. The Rock Pigeon (p. 241) has colorful iridescent patches. Look for the black collar on the nape and the squared tail to help identify the Eurasian Collared-Dove.

**Stan's Notes:** This non-native bird has spread across Missouri, having moved into Florida in the early 1980s after inadvertent introduction to the Bahamas. It has been expanding its range across North America and is predicted to spread just like it did through Europe from Asia. Unknown how this "new" bird will affect populations of the native Mourning Dove. Nearly identical to the Ringed Turtle-Dove, a common pet bird. The dark mark on the back of the neck gave rise to the common name. Look for flashes of white in the tail and dark wing tips when it lands or takes off.

# Rock Pigeon
*Columba livia*

**YEAR-ROUND**

| | |
|---|---|
| **Size:** | 13" (33 cm) |
| **Male:** | No set color pattern. Shades of gray to white with patches of gleaming, iridescent green and blue. Often has a light rump patch. |
| **Female:** | same as male |
| **Juvenile:** | same as adults |
| **Nest:** | platform; female builds; 3–4 broods per year |
| **Eggs:** | 1–2; white without markings |
| **Incubation:** | 18–20 days; female and male incubate |
| **Fledging:** | 25–26 days; female and male feed the young |
| **Migration:** | non-migrator |
| **Food:** | seeds |
| **Compare:** | The Eurasian Collared-Dove (p. 239) has a black collar on the nape. The Mourning Dove (p. 163) is smaller and light brown and lacks the variety of color combinations of the Rock Pigeon. |

**Stan's Notes:** Also known as the Domestic Pigeon. Formerly known as the Rock Dove. Introduced to North America from Europe by the early settlers. Most common around cities and barnyards, where it scratches for seeds. One of the few birds with a wide variety of colors, produced by years of selective breeding while in captivity. Parents feed the young a regurgitated liquid known as crop-milk for the first few days of life. One of the few birds that can drink without tilting its head back. Nests under bridges or on buildings, balconies, barns and sheds. Was once thought to be a nuisance in cities and was poisoned. Now, many cities have Peregrine Falcons (p. 245) feeding on Rock Pigeons, which keeps their numbers in check.

soaring

juvenile

# Cooper's Hawk
*Accipiter cooperii*

YEAR-ROUND

**Size:** 14–20" (36–51 cm); up to 3' wingspan

**Male:** Medium-size hawk with short wings and a long, rounded tail with several black bands. Slate-gray back, rusty breast, dark wing tips. Gray bill with a bright-yellow spot at the base. Dark-red eyes.

**Female:** similar to male but larger

**Juvenile:** brown back, brown streaking on the breast, bright-yellow eyes

**Nest:** platform; male and female construct; 1 brood per year

**Eggs:** 2–4; greenish with brown markings

**Incubation:** 32–36 days; female and male incubate

**Fledging:** 28–32 days; male and female feed the young

**Migration:** non-migrator to partial migrator; southern states and Mexico

**Food:** small birds, mammals

**Compare:** Sharp-shinned Hawk (p. 235) is much smaller, lighter gray and has a squared tail. Look for the banded, rounded tail to help identify Cooper's Hawk.

**Stan's Notes:** Found in many habitats, from woodlands to parks and backyards. Stubby wings help it to navigate around trees while it chases small birds. Will ambush prey, flying into heavy brush or even running on the ground. Comes to feeders, hunting for birds. Flies with long glides followed by a few quick flaps. Calls a loud, clear "cack-cack-cack-cack." The young have gray eyes that turn bright yellow at 1 year and turn dark red later, after 3–5 years.

243

juvenile

in-flight
juvenile

in flight

# Peregrine Falcon
*Falco peregrinus*

SUMMER MIGRATION

**Size:** 16–20" (41–51 cm); up to 3¾' wingspan

**Male:** Dark-gray back and tan-to-white chest. Horizontal bars on belly, legs and undertail. Dark "hood" head marking and wide black mustache. Yellow base of bill and eye-ring. Yellow legs.

**Female:** similar to male but noticeably larger

**Juvenile:** overall darker than adults, with heavy streaking on the chest and belly

**Nest:** ground (scrape) on a cliff edge, tall building, bridge or smokestack; 1 brood per year

**Eggs:** 3–4; white, some with brown markings

**Incubation:** 29–32 days; female and male incubate

**Fledging:** 35–42 days; male and female feed the young

**Migration:** complete, to southern states

**Food:** birds (Rock Pigeons in cities; shorebirds and waterfowl in rural areas)

**Compare:** The American Kestrel (p. 147) is smaller and has 2 vertical black stripes on its face. Look for the dark "hood" head marking and mustache marks to identify the Peregrine Falcon.

**Stan's Notes:** A wide-bodied raptor that hunts many bird species. The larger females hunt larger prey. Lives in many cities, diving (stooping) on pigeons at speeds of up to 200 miles (322 km) per hour, which knocks them to the ground. Soars with its wings flat, often riding thermals. During courtship, the male brings food to the female and performs aerial displays. Likes to nest on a high ledge or platform for a good view of its territory. A solitary nester and monogamous.

male

female
p. 189

soaring

YEAR-ROUND
WINTER

# Northern Harrier
*Circus hudsonius*

**Size:** 18–22" (45–56 cm); up to 4' wingspan

**Male:** Slender, low-flying hawk. Silver-gray with a large white rump patch and white belly. Long tail with faint narrow bands. Black wing tips. Yellow eyes.

**Female:** dark-brown back, brown streaking on breast and belly, large white rump patch, thin, black tail bands, black wing tips, yellow eyes

**Juvenile:** similar to female, with an orange breast

**Nest:** ground; female and male construct; 1 brood per year

**Eggs:** 4–8; bluish white without markings

**Incubation:** 31–32 days; female incubates

**Fledging:** 30–35 days; male and female feed the young

**Migration:** partial migrator, to southern states, Mexico and Central America; winters in Missouri

**Food:** mice, snakes, insects, small birds

**Compare:** Slimmer than the Red-tailed Hawk (p. 191). Cooper's Hawk (p. 243) has a rusty breast. Look for a low-gliding hawk with a large white rump patch to identify the male Harrier.

**Stan's Notes:** One of the easiest of hawks to identify. Glides just above the ground, following the contours of the land while searching for prey. Holds its wings just above horizontal, tilting back and forth in the wind, similar to Turkey Vultures. Formerly called the Marsh Hawk due to its habit of hunting over marshes. Feeds and nests on the ground. Will also preen and rest on the ground. Unlike other hawks, mainly uses its hearing to find prey, followed by sight. At any age, has a distinctive owl-like face disk.

male

female
p. 181

# Gadwall
*Mareca strepera*

WINTER

**Size:** 19" (48 cm)

**Male:** A plump gray duck with a brown head and a distinctive black rump. White belly. Chestnut-tinged wings. Bright-white wing linings. Small white wing patch, seen when swimming. Gray bill.

**Female:** similar to female Mallard, a mottled brown with a pronounced color change from dark-brown body to light-brown neck and head, bright-white wing linings, small white wing patch, gray bill with orange sides

**Juvenile:** similar to female

**Nest:** ground; female lines the nest with fine grass and down feathers plucked from her chest; 1 brood per year

**Eggs:** 8–11; white without markings

**Incubation:** 24–27 days; female incubates

**Fledging:** 48–56 days; young feed themselves

**Migration:** complete, to Missouri, southern states and Mexico

**Food:** aquatic insects

**Compare:** Male Gadwall is one of the few gray ducks. Look for its distinctive black rump.

**Stan's Notes:** A duck of shallow marshes. Consumes mostly plant material, dunking its head in water to feed rather than tipping forward, like other dabbling ducks. Walks well on land; feeds in fields and woodlands. Frequently in pairs with other duck species. Nests within 300 feet (90 m) of water. Establishes pair bond in winter.

in flight

# Canada Goose
*Branta canadensis*

YEAR-ROUND

**Size:** 25–43" (64–109 cm); up to 5½' wingspan

**Male:** Large gray goose with a black neck and head. White chin and cheek strap.

**Female:** same as male

**Juvenile:** same as adults

**Nest:** platform, on the ground; female builds; 1 brood per year

**Eggs:** 5–10; white without markings

**Incubation:** 25–30 days; female incubates

**Fledging:** 42–55 days; male and female teach the young to feed

**Migration:** non-migrator

**Food:** aquatic plants, insects, seeds

**Compare:** Rarely confused with any other bird.

**Stan's Notes:** Formerly killed off (extirpated) in Missouri, it was reintroduced in the 1940–50s and is now a common year-round resident. Adapting to our changed environment very well, it breeds throughout the state. Calls a classic "honk-honk-honk," especially in flight. Flocks fly in a large V when traveling long distances. Begins breeding in the third year. Adults mate for many years. If threatened, they will hiss as a warning. Males stand as sentinels at the edge of their group and will bob their heads and become aggressive if approached. Adults molt their primary flight feathers while raising their young, rendering family groups temporarily flightless. Several subspecies vary in the U.S. Generally eastern groups are paler than western. Their size also varies, decreasing northward. The smallest subspecies is in the Arctic.

in flight

# Great Blue Heron
*Ardea herodias*

YEAR-ROUND
SUMMER

**Size:** 42–48" (107–122 cm); up to 6' wingspan

**Male:** Tall and gray. Black eyebrows end in long plumes at the back of the head. Long, yellow bill. Long feathers at the base of the neck drop down in a kind of necklace. Long legs.

**Female:** same as male

**Juvenile:** same as adults, but more brown than gray, with a black crown; lacks plumes

**Nest:** platform in a colony; male and female build; 1 brood per year

**Eggs:** 3–5; blue-green without markings

**Incubation:** 27–28 days; female and male incubate

**Fledging:** 56–60 days; male and female feed the young

**Migration:** complete, to southern states, Mexico, and Central and South America; non-migrator in southern Missouri

**Food:** small fish, frogs, insects, snakes, baby birds

**Compare:** The Great Egret (p. 295) is similar in shape, but it's smaller and all white.

**Stan's Notes:** One of the most common herons. Found in open water, from small ponds to large lakes. Stalks small fish in shallow water. Will strike at mice, squirrels and nearly anything it comes across. Red-winged Blackbirds will attack it to stop it from taking their babies out of the nest. In flight, it holds its neck in an S shape and slightly cups its wings, while the legs trail straight out behind. Nests in a colony of up to 100 birds. Nests in trees near or hanging over water. Barks like a dog when startled.

in flight

rusty stain

in-flight
rusty stain

# Ruby-throated Hummingbird
*Archilochus colubris*

SUMMER

**Size:** 3–3½" (7.5–9 cm)

**Male:** Tiny iridescent green bird with black throat patch that reflects bright ruby red in sun.

**Female:** same as male, but lacking the throat patch

**Juvenile:** same as female

**Nest:** cup; female builds; 1–2 broods per year

**Eggs:** 2; white without markings

**Incubation:** 12–14 days; female incubates

**Fledging:** 14–18 days; female feeds the young

**Migration:** complete, to southern states, Mexico and Central America

**Food:** nectar, insects; will come to nectar feeders

**Compare:** No other bird is as tiny. The Sphinx Moth also hovers at flowers but has clear wings, doesn't hum in flight, moves much slower than the Ruby-throated and can be approached.

**Stan's Notes:** This is the smallest bird in Missouri. Can fly straight up, straight down or backward and hover in midair. Does not sing but chatters or buzzes to communicate. Weighs about the same as a U.S. penny; it takes about five average-sized hummingbirds to equal the weight of one chickadee. The wings create the humming sound. Flaps 50–60 times or more per second when flying at top speed. Breathes 250 times per minute. Heart beats up to 1,260 times per minute. Builds a stretchy nest with plant material and spiderwebs, gluing pieces of lichen to the exterior for camouflage. Attracted to colorful, tubular flowers. Will extract and eat insects trapped in spiderwebs.

in flight

# Green Heron
*Butorides virescens*

SUMMER

**Size:** 16–22" (41–56 cm)

**Male:** Short and stocky. Blue-green back and rust-red neck and breast. Dark-green crest. Short legs are normally yellow but turn bright orange during the breeding season.

**Female:** same as male

**Juvenile:** similar to adults, with a bluish-gray back and white-streaked breast and neck

**Nest:** platform; female and male build; 2 broods per year

**Eggs:** 2–4; light green without markings

**Incubation:** 21–25 days; female and male incubate

**Fledging:** 35–36 days; female and male feed the young

**Migration:** complete, to southern states, Mexico and Central and South America

**Food:** small fish, aquatic insects, small amphibians

**Compare:** Great Blue Heron (p. 253) is larger. Green Heron lacks the long neck of other herons. Look for a small heron with a dark-green back and crest to identify the Green.

**Stan's Notes:** Often gives an explosive, rasping "skyew" call when startled. Holds its head close to its body, which sometimes makes it look like it doesn't have a neck. Waits on the shore or wades stealthily, hunting for small fish, aquatic insects and small amphibians. Places an object, such as an insect, on the water's surface to attract fish to catch. Nests in a tall tree, often a short distance from the water. The nest can be very high up in the tree. Babies give a loud ticking sound, like the ticktock of a clock.

female
p. 179

male

YEAR-ROUND
SUMMER

# Wood Duck
*Aix sponsa*

| | |
|---|---|
| **Size:** | 17–20" (43–51 cm) |
| **Male:** | Small, highly ornamented dabbling duck. Mostly green head and crest patterned with black and white. Rusty chest and a white belly. Red eyes. |
| **Female:** | brown duck with a bright-white eye-ring, not-so-obvious crest, and blue patch on wings (speculum), often hidden |
| **Juvenile:** | similar to female |
| **Nest:** | cavity; female lines an old woodpecker cavity or a nest box in a tree; 1 brood per year |
| **Eggs:** | 10–15; creamy white without markings |
| **Incubation:** | 28–36 days; female incubates |
| **Fledging:** | 56–68 days; female teaches the young to feed |
| **Migration:** | complete, to southern states; non-migrator in southern Missouri |
| **Food:** | aquatic insects, plants, seeds |
| **Compare:** | Male Northern Shoveler (p. 265) is larger with a long, wide bill. |

**Stan's Notes:** A duck of quiet, shallow backwater ponds. Nearly extinct around 1900 due to overhunting, but doing well now. Nests in tree cavity or nest box. Seen flying in forests or perching on high branches. Female takes off with a loud squealing call and enters the nest cavity from full flight. Lays some eggs in a neighboring nest (egg dumping), resulting in more than 20 eggs in some clutches. Hatchlings stay in nest for 24 hours, then jump from as high as 60 feet (18 m) to the ground or water to follow their mother. They never return to the nest.

male

female
p. 183

# Northern Shoveler

*Spatula clypeata*

MIGRATION
WINTER

| | |
|---|---|
| **Size:** | 19–21" (48–53 cm) |
| **Male:** | Medium-sized duck with an iridescent green head, rust sides, white chest. Extraordinarily large, spoon-shaped bill, almost always held pointed toward the water. |
| **Female:** | brown and black all over, green wing patch (speculum) and a large spoon-shaped bill |
| **Juvenile:** | same as female |
| **Nest:** | ground; female builds; 1 brood per year |
| **Eggs:** | 9–12; olive without markings |
| **Incubation:** | 22–25 days; female incubates |
| **Fledging:** | 30–60 days; female leads the young to food |
| **Migration:** | complete, to southern states, Mexico, Central America; winters in southern Missouri |
| **Food:** | aquatic insects, plants |
| **Compare:** | Male Mallard (p. 263) is similar, but it lacks the large spoon-shaped bill. The male Wood Duck (p. 261) is smaller and has a crest. |

**Stan's Notes:** One of several species of shovelers. Called "Shoveler" due to the peculiar, shovel-like shape of its bill. Given the common name "Northern" because it is the only species of these ducks in North America. Seen in shallow wetlands, ponds and small lakes in flocks of 5–10 birds. Flocks fly in tight formation. Swims low in water, pointing its large bill toward the water as if it's too heavy to lift. Usually swims in tight circles while feeding. Feeds mainly by filtering tiny aquatic insects and plants from the surface of the water with its bill. Female gathers plant material and forms it into a nest a short distance from the water.

in flight

female
p. 285

male

WINTER

# Common Merganser
*Merqus merganser*

**Size:** 26–28" (66–71 cm)

**Male:** Long, thin, duck-like bird with a green head and black back. White sides, chest and neck. Long, pointed orange bill. Often looks black and white in poor light.

**Female:** same size and shape as the male, with a rust-red head and ragged "hair," gray body, white chest and chin

**Juvenile:** same as female

**Nest:** cavity; female lines an old woodpecker hole or a natural cavity; 1 brood per year

**Eggs:** 9–11; ivory without markings

**Incubation:** 28–33 days; female incubates

**Fledging:** 70–80 days; female feeds the young

**Migration:** complete migrator; winters in Missouri

**Food:** small fish, aquatic insects, amphibians

**Compare:** The male Mallard (p. 263) is smaller and lacks the black back and long, pointed orange bill.

**Stan's Notes:** Seen on any open water during the winter but more common along large rivers than lakes. A large, shallow-water diver that feeds on fish in 10–15 feet (3–4.5 m) of water. Bill has a fine, serrated-like edge that helps catch slippery fish. Female often lays some eggs in other merganser nests (egg dumping), resulting in up to 15 young in some broods. Male leaves female once she starts incubating. Orphans are accepted by other merganser mothers with young. Fast flight, often low and close to the water, in groups but not in formation. Usually not vocal except for an alarm call.

female
p. 307

male

# American Redstart
*Setophaga ruticilla*

SUMMER

| | |
|---|---|
| **Size:** | 5" (13 cm) |
| **Male:** | Striking black warbler with orange patches on the sides, wings and tail. White belly. |
| **Female:** | olive-brown with yellow patches on the sides, wings and tail, white belly |
| **Juvenile:** | same as female; male attains orange tinges in the second year |
| **Nest:** | cup; female builds; 1 brood per year |
| **Eggs:** | 3–5; off-white with brown markings |
| **Incubation:** | 12 days; female incubates |
| **Fledging:** | 9 days; female and male feed the young |
| **Migration:** | complete, to Mexico, Central America and South America |
| **Food:** | insects, seeds, occasionally berries |
| **Compare:** | The male Baltimore Oriole (p. 271) and male Red-winged Blackbird (p. 31) are much larger. The male American Redstart is the only small black-and-orange bird flitting around the top of trees. |

**Stan's Notes:** Common and widespread warbler in Missouri that prefers large, unbroken tracts of forest. Found in woodlands, parks and yards and at forest edges. Appears hyperactive when it feeds, hovering and darting back and forth to glean insects from leaves. Often droops wings and fans tail before launching out to catch an insect. Look for the flashing black-and-orange colors of the male high up in trees. First-year males have yellow markings and look like the females. Sings a high-pitched song that builds in intensity and then suddenly ends.

female
p. 313

male

SUMMER

# Baltimore Oriole
*Icterus galbula*

**Size:** 7–8" (18–20 cm)

**Male:** Flaming orange with a black head and back. White-and-orange wing bars. Orange-and-black tail. Gray bill and dark eyes.

**Female:** pale yellow with orange tones, gray-brown wings, white wing bars, gray bill, dark eyes

**Juvenile:** same as female

**Nest:** pendulous; female builds; 1 brood per year

**Eggs:** 4–5; bluish with brown markings

**Incubation:** 12–14 days; female incubates

**Fledging:** 12–14 days; female and male feed the young

**Migration:** complete, to Mexico, Central America and South America

**Food:** insects, fruit, nectar; comes to nectar, orange-half, and grape-jelly feeders

**Compare:** The male Orchard Oriole (p. 273) is much darker orange. Look for the flaming orange to identify the male Baltimore Oriole.

**Stan's Notes:** A fantastic songster, often heard before seen. Easily attracted to a feeder that offers sugar water (nectar), orange halves, or grape jelly. Parents bring their young to feeders. Sits at the tops of trees, feeding on caterpillars. Female builds a sock-like nest at the outermost branches of tall trees. Prefers parks, yards and forests and often returns to the same area year after year. Young males turn orange-and-black at 1½ years of age. Some of the last birds to arrive in spring (March/April) and first to leave in fall (August).

female
p. 315

male

first-year
male

# Orchard Oriole
*Icterus spurius*

SUMMER

**Size:** 7–8" (18–20 cm)

**Male:** Dark orange with black head, throat, upper back, wings and tail. White wing bar. Bill is long and thin. Gray mark on lower bill.

**Female:** olive-green back, dull-yellow belly and gray wings with 2 indistinct white wing bars

**Juvenile:** same as female; first-year male looks like the female, with a black bib

**Nest:** pendulous; female builds; 1 brood per year

**Eggs:** 3–5; pale blue to white, brown markings

**Incubation:** 11–12 days; female and male incubate

**Fledging:** 11–14 days; female and male feed the young

**Migration:** complete, to central Mexico, Central America and northern South America

**Food:** insects, fruit, nectar; comes to nectar, orange-half, and grape-jelly feeders

**Compare:** The male Baltimore Oriole (p. 271) is brighter orange. Look for the dark-orange plumage to identify the male Orchard Oriole.

**Stan's Notes:** Named "Orchard" for its preference for orchards. Also likes open woods. Eats insects until wild fruit starts to ripen. Often nests alone; sometimes nests in small colonies. Parents bring their young to bird feeding stations after they fledge. Many people don't see these birds at their feeders very much during the summer and think they have left, but the birds are still there, hunting for insects to feed to their young. One of the last birds to arrive in spring and one of the first to leave in fall. Spends 4–5 months in Missouri. Often migrates in flocks with Baltimore Orioles.

male

female
p. 91

yellow
male

# House Finch
*Haemorhous mexicanus*

YEAR-ROUND

**Size:** 5" (13 cm)

**Male:** Small finch with a red-to-orange face, throat, chest and rump. Brown cap. Brown marking behind eyes. White belly with brown streaks. Brown wings with white streaks.

**Female:** brown with a heavily streaked white chest

**Juvenile:** similar to female

**Nest:** cup, sometimes in cavities; female builds; 2 broods per year

**Eggs:** 4–5; pale blue, lightly marked

**Incubation:** 12–14 days; female incubates

**Fledging:** 15–19 days; female and male feed the young

**Migration:** non-migrator to partial migrator; moves around to find food

**Food:** seeds, fruit, leaf buds; visits seed feeders and feeders that offer grape jelly

**Compare:** The male Purple Finch (p. 277) is very similar, but male House Finch lacks the red cap. Look for the brown cap and streaked belly to help identify the male House Finch.

**Stan's Notes:** Can be a common bird at your feeders. Very social, visiting feeders in small flocks. Likes to nest in hanging flower baskets. Male sings a loud, cheerful warbling song. It was originally introduced to Long Island, New York, from the western U.S. in the 1940s and is now found throughout the country. Suffers from a disease that causes the eyes to crust, resulting in blindness and death. Rarely, males are yellow (inset), perhaps due to poor diet.

female
p. 111

male

# Purple Finch
*Haemorhous purpureus*

WINTER

| | |
|---|---|
| **Size:** | 6" (15 cm) |
| **Male:** | Raspberry-red head, cap, chest, back and rump. Brownish wings and tail. Large bill. |
| **Female:** | heavily streaked brown-and-white bird with bold white eyebrows |
| **Juvenile:** | same as female |
| **Nest:** | cup; female and male build; 1 brood per year |
| **Eggs:** | 4–5; greenish blue with brown markings |
| **Incubation:** | 12–13 days; female incubates |
| **Fledging:** | 13–14 days; female and male feed the young |
| **Migration:** | irruptive; moves around in search of food |
| **Food:** | seeds, insects, fruit; comes to seed feeders |
| **Compare:** | The male House Finch (p. 275) has a brown cap and a streaked belly. Look for the raspberry cap to help identify the male Purple Finch. |

**Stan's Notes:** Usually seen only during migration and in winter, when flocks of Purple Finches leave their homes farther north and move around searching for food. Travels in flocks of up to 50 birds. Visits seed feeders along with House Finches, which makes it hard to tell them apart. Feeds mainly on seeds; ash tree seeds are an important source of food. Found in coniferous forests, mixed woods, woodland edges and suburban backyards. Flies in the typical undulating, up-and-down pattern of finches. Sings a rich, loud song. Gives a distinctive "tic" note only in flight. Male is not purple. The Latin species name *purpureus* means "purple" (or other reddish colors).

female
p. 311

male

# Scarlet Tanager
*Piranga olivacea*

SUMMER

| | |
|---|---|
| **Size:** | 7" (18 cm) |
| **Male:** | Bright scarlet with coal-black wings and tail. Ivory bill and dark eyes. |
| **Female:** | drab greenish yellow with olive wings and tail, whitish wing linings and dark eyes |
| **Juvenile:** | same as female |
| **Nest:** | cup; female builds; 1 brood per year |
| **Eggs:** | 4–5; blue-green with brown markings |
| **Incubation:** | 13–14 days; female incubates |
| **Fledging:** | 9–11 days; female and male feed the young |
| **Migration:** | complete, to Central and South America |
| **Food:** | insects, fruit |
| **Compare:** | Male Summer Tanager (p. 281) is slightly larger and rosy red in color vs. the scarlet red of male Scarlet Tanager. The male Northern Cardinal (p. 283) is larger, with a black mask and red bill. |

**Stan's Notes:** A tropical-looking bird. Found in mature deciduous woodlands, where it hunts for insects high up in trees. Requires a territory covering at least 4 acres (1.5 ha) for nesting but prefers 8 acres (3 ha). Arrives late in spring and leaves early in fall. Male and female both sing like American Robins, but the tanagers intersperse an unusual "chick-burr" call in their songs. The song of the female is like that of the male, only softer. This bird is one of hundreds of tanager species in the world. Nearly all are brightly colored and live in the tropics. The name "Tanager" comes from a South American Tupi Indian word meaning "any small, brightly colored bird." The male sheds (molts) his bright-scarlet plumage in the fall, appearing more like the female during winter.

female
p. 317

male

SUMMER

# Summer Tanager
*Piranga rubra*

| | |
|---|---|
| **Size:** | 8" (20 cm) |
| **Male:** | Bright rosy-red bird with darker red wings. |
| **Female:** | overall yellow with slightly darker wings |
| **Juvenile:** | male has patches of red and green over the entire body, female is same as adult female |
| **Nest:** | cup; female builds; 1–2 broods per year |
| **Eggs:** | 3–5; pale blue with dark markings |
| **Incubation:** | 10–12 days; female incubates |
| **Fledging:** | 12–15 days; female and male feed young |
| **Migration:** | complete, to Central and South America |
| **Food:** | insects, fruit |
| **Compare:** | Slightly larger than the male Scarlet Tanager (p. 279), which is scarlet red with black wings, compared with the rosy color of the male Summer Tanager. Similar size as male Northern Cardinal (p. 283), but Cardinal has a black mask, large crest and red bill. |

**Stan's Notes:** Found throughout the summer in Missouri forests, especially in mixed hickory-oak woods. Due to clearing of land for agriculture, populations have decreased for over a century and especially most recently. Returning to the state in late April and with young hatching in late May, some pairs have two broods per year. While fruit makes up some of the diet, most of it consists of insects such as bees and wasps. More common in Missouri than Scarlet Tanagers. Summer Tanagers unfortunately seem to be parasitized by Brown-headed Cowbirds.

female
p. 141

male

juvenile

YEAR-ROUND

# Northern Cardinal
*Cardinalis cardinalis*

**Size:** 8–9" (20–23 cm)

**Male:** Red with a black mask that extends from the face to the throat. Large crest and a large red bill.

**Female:** buff-brown with a black mask, large reddish bill, and red tinges on the crest and wings

**Juvenile:** same as female but with a blackish-gray bill

**Nest:** cup; female builds; 2–3 broods per year

**Eggs:** 3–4; bluish white with brown markings

**Incubation:** 12–13 days; female and male incubate

**Fledging:** 9–10 days; female and male feed the young

**Migration:** non-migrator

**Food:** seeds, insects, fruit; comes to seed feeders

**Compare:** Similar size as the male Summer Tanager (p. 281), but the male Tanager is rosy red. Male Scarlet Tanager (p. 279) has black wings and tail. Look for the black mask, large crest and red bill to identify the male Northern Cardinal.

**Stan's Notes:** A familiar backyard bird. Seen in a variety of habitats, including parks. Usually likes thick vegetation. One of the few species in which both males and females sing. Can be heard all year. Listen for its "whata-cheer-cheer-cheer" territorial call in spring. Watch for a male feeding a female during courtship. The male also feeds the young of the first brood while the female builds a second nest. Territorial in spring, fighting its own reflection in a window or other reflective surface. Non-territorial in winter, gathering in small flocks of up to 20 birds. *Cardinalis* denotes importance, as represented by the red priestly garments of Catholic cardinals.

**in flight**

**male**
**p. 267**

**female**

# Common Merganser

*Mergus merganser*

**Size:** 26–28" (66–71 cm)

**Female:** Long, thin, duck-like bird with a rust-red head and ragged "hair." Gray body and white chest and chin. Long, pointed orange bill.

**Male:** same size and shape as the female, but with a green head, a black back and white sides

**Juvenile:** same as female

**Nest:** cavity; female lines an old woodpecker hole or a natural cavity; 1 brood per year

**Eggs:** 9–11; ivory without markings

**Incubation:** 28–33 days; female incubates

**Fledging:** 70–80 days; female feeds the young

**Migration:** complete, to southern states and Mexico; winters in Missouri

**Food:** small fish, aquatic insects

**Compare:** Hard to confuse with other birds. Look for a rust-red head with ragged "hair," a white chin and a long, pointed orange bill to identify.

**Stan's Notes:** Seen on any open water during the winter but more common along large rivers than lakes. A large, shallow-water diver that feeds on fish in 10–15 feet (3–4.5 m) of water. Bill has a fine, serrated-like edge that helps catch slippery fish. The female often lays some eggs in other merganser nests (egg dumping), resulting in up to 15 young in some broods. Male leaves the female once she starts incubating. Orphans are accepted by other merganser mothers with young. Fast flight, often low and close to the water, in groups but not in formation. Usually not vocal except for an alarm call that sounds like a muffled quack.

in flight

breeding

juvenile

winter

# Ring-billed Gull
*Larus delawarensis*

MIGRATION
WINTER

**Size:** 18–20" (45–51 cm); up to 4' wingspan

**Male:** White with gray wings, black wing tips spotted with white, and a white tail, seen in flight (inset). Yellow bill with a black ring near the tip. Yellowish legs and feet. In winter, the back of the head and the nape of the neck are speckled brown.

**Female:** same as male

**Juvenile:** white with brown speckles and a brown tip of tail; mostly dark bill

**Nest:** ground; female and male construct; 1 brood per year

**Eggs:** 2–4; off-white with brown markings

**Incubation:** 20–21 days; female and male incubate

**Fledging:** 20–40 days; female and male feed the young

**Migration:** complete, to southern states and Mexico; winters in southern third of Missouri and along the Mississippi River

**Food:** insects, fish; scavenges for food

**Compare:** White and gray gull occurring in winter in Missouri. Look for a black ring near the tip of yellow bill, and yellow legs and feet.

**Stan's Notes:** A common gull of garbage dumps and parking lots. One of the most common gulls in the U.S. Hundreds of these birds often flock together. A three-year gull with different plumages in each of its first three years. Attains the ring on its bill after the first winter and adult plumage in the third year. Defends a small area around the nest, usually only a few feet.

in flight

# Cattle Egret
*Bubulcus ibis*

SUMMER
MIGRATION

**Size:** 18–22" (45–56 cm); up to 3' wingspan

**Male:** White with orange-buff crest, breast and back. Stocky with a disproportionally large round head. Red-orange bill and legs. Winter plumage is all white with a yellow bill and dark legs.

**Female:** same as male

**Juvenile:** similar to winter adult but with a dark bill

**Nest:** platform; female and male build; 1 brood per year

**Eggs:** 2–5; light blue-green without markings

**Incubation:** 22–26 days; female and male incubate

**Fledging:** 28–30 days; female and male feed the young

**Migration:** complete migrator, to southern states, Mexico, Central and South America; will move around to find food

**Food:** insects, small mammals

**Compare:** Great Egret (p. 295) is about twice as large and has a much longer neck and a much larger bill.

**Stan's Notes:** Came to South America from Africa around 1880, reaching Florida in the 1940s. Started being seen in Missouri in the mid-1960s. Often seen solo in pastures, hunting insects at cow and horse pies by wiggling its neck and head back and forth and from side to side, while holding its body still. Then it stabs at prey and tosses it to the back of its mouth. Frequently attracted to field fires to hunt newly exposed animals and insects. In some years it is found as far as northern-tier states and Canada.

in flight

# Snowy Egret
*Egretta thula*

SUMMER MIGRATION

**Size:** 22–26" (56–66 cm); up to 3½' wingspan

**Male:** All-white bird with black bill. Black legs. Bright-yellow feet. Long feather plumes on head, neck and back during breeding season.

**Female:** same as male

**Juvenile:** similar to adult, but backs of legs are yellow

**Nest:** platform; female and male build; 1 brood per year

**Eggs:** 3–5; light blue-green without markings

**Incubation:** 20–24 days; female and male incubate

**Fledging:** 28–30 days; female and male feed the young

**Migration:** complete, to southern coastal states and Mexico

**Food:** aquatic insects, small fish

**Compare:** Great Egret (p. 295) is much larger and has a yellow bill and black feet. Look for the black bill and yellow feet of Snowy Egret to help identify.

**Stan's Notes:** Common in wetlands and often seen with other egrets. Colonies may include up to several hundred nests. Nests are low in shrubs 5–10 feet (1.5–3 m) tall or constructs a nest on the ground, usually mixed among other egret and heron nests. Chicks hatch days apart (asynchronous), leading to starvation of last to hatch. Will actively "hunt" prey by moving around quickly, stirring up small fish and aquatic insects with its feet. In the breeding state, a yellow patch at the base of bill and the yellow feet turn orange-red. Was hunted to near extinction in the late 1800s for its feathers.

blue morph

juvenile

white
morph

in flight

# Snow Goose
*Anser caerulescens*

**Size:** 25–38" (64–97 cm); up to 4½' wingspan

**Male:** White morph has black wing tips and varying patches of black and brown. Blue morph has a white head and a gray breast and back. Both morphs have a pink bill and legs.

**Female:** same as male

**Juvenile:** overall dull gray with a dark bill

**Nest:** ground; female builds; 1 brood per year

**Eggs:** 3–5; white without markings

**Incubation:** 23–25 days; female incubates

**Fledging:** 45–49 days; female and male teach the young to feed

**Migration:** complete, to New Mexico and California, southern states and Mexico

**Food:** aquatic insects and plants

**Compare:** The Canada Goose (p. 251) is larger and has a black neck and chin strap. The American White Pelican (p. 299) shares black wing tips, but it has an enormous bill.

**Stan's Notes:** This bird occurs in light (white) and dark (blue) color morphs. The white morph is more common than the blue. A bird of wide-open fields, wetlands and lakes of any size. It has a thick, serrated bill, which helps it to grab and pull up plants. Breeds in large colonies on the northern tundra in Canada. Female starts to breed at 2–3 years. Older females produce more eggs and are more successful at reproduction than younger females. Seen by the thousands during migration and in winter. Commonly seen with Sandhill Cranes. Has a classic goose-like call.

in flight

SUMMER

# Great Egret
*Ardea alba*

**Size:** 36–40" (91–102 cm); up to 4½' wingspan

**Male:** Tall, thin, all-white bird with a long neck and a long, pointed yellow bill. Black, stilt-like legs and black feet.

**Female:** same as male

**Juvenile:** same as adults

**Nest:** platform; male and female construct; 1 brood per year

**Eggs:** 2–3; light blue without markings

**Incubation:** 23–26 days; female and male incubate

**Fledging:** 43–49 days; female and male feed the young

**Migration:** complete, to southern states, Mexico and Central America

**Food:** small fish, aquatic insects, frogs, crayfish

**Compare:** Cattle Egret (p. 289) is about half the size of Great Egret and has a much shorter neck and much smaller bill. The Snowy Egret (p. 291) is much smaller, with yellow feet and a black bill.

**Stan's Notes:** Slowly stalks shallow ponds, lakes and wetlands in search of small fish to spear with its long, sharp bill. Gives a loud, dry croak if disturbed or when squabbling for a nest site at the colony. The name "Egret" comes from the French word *aigrette*, meaning "ornamental tufts of plumes." The plumes grow near the tail during the breeding season. Hunted to near extinction in the 1800s and early 1900s for its long plumes, which were used to decorate women's hats. Today, the egret is a protected species.

in flight

juvenile

# Trumpeter Swan
*Cygnus buccinator*

MIGRATION
WINTER

**Size:** 58–62" (147–157 cm); up to 6½' wingspan

**Male:** A large, all-white swan with an all-black bill, legs and feet.

**Female:** same as male

**Juvenile:** same size as adult, with gray plumage and a pinkish-gray bill

**Nest:** ground; female and male construct; 1 brood per year

**Eggs:** 4–6; cream-white without markings

**Incubation:** 33–37 days; female incubates

**Fledging:** 100–120 days; female and male show the young what to eat

**Migration:** complete migrator; winters in Missouri

**Food:** aquatic plants, insects

**Compare:** Snow Goose (p. 293) is much smaller and has black wing tips.

**Stan's Notes:** Was once eliminated from the Lower 48 states due to market hunting but reintroduced with great success. Most breeding programs were started with eggs taken from Trumpeters in Alaska. Often on larger rivers. Also in wetlands, marshes, small lakes, ponds and farm fields. Gathers in large numbers on any open water or major rivers during winter. Mated pairs defend large territories and construct large mound nests at the edge of water. Named for its loud, trumpet-like call, typically given in flight. Healthy populations in Minnesota and Wisconsin migrate to Missouri each winter.

breeding

in flight

chick-feeding adult

# American White Pelican
*Pelecanus erythrorhynchos*

SUMMER
MIGRATION
WINTER

**Size:** 60–64" (152–163 cm); up to 9' wingspan

**Male:** Large white pelican with an enormous bright-yellow-to-orange bill. Yellow legs and feet. Black wing tips and trailing edge of wings. Breeding plumage has a bright-orange bill, legs and feet. Chick-feeding adult (an adult that is feeding young) has a gray-black crown.

**Female:** same as male

**Juvenile:** duller white than adult, with a brownish head and neck

**Nest:** ground, scraped-out depression rimmed with dirt; female and male build; 1 brood per year

**Eggs:** 1–3; white without markings

**Incubation:** 29–36 days; male and female incubate

**Fledging:** 60–70 days; female and male feed the young

**Migration:** complete, to southern coastal states, Mexico and Central America

**Food:** fish

**Compare:** Snow Goose (p. 293) is much smaller and lacks the Pelican's enormous bill. Look for American White Pelican's black wing tips in flight.

**Stan's Notes:** Often seen in large groups on the larger lakes and rivers. Doesn't dive to catch fish, like coastal Brown Pelicans (not shown). Instead, groups swim and dip their bills simultaneously into water to scoop up fish. Groups fly in a large V, often gliding, followed by simultaneous flapping. Large flocks swirl on columns of rising warm air (thermals) on hot days. Breeding adults typically grow a flat, fibrous plate on the upper bill, which drops off after the eggs hatch. Usually silent; gives short grunts at the nesting colony.

male

winter
male

female

# American Goldfinch

*Spinus tristis*

**Size:** 5" (13 cm)

**Male:** Canary-yellow finch with a black forehead and tail. Black wings with white wing bars. White rump. No markings on the chest. Winter male is similar to the female.

**Female:** dull olive-yellow plumage with brown wings; lacks a black forehead

**Juvenile:** same as female

**Nest:** cup; female builds; 1 brood per year

**Eggs:** 4–6; pale blue without markings

**Incubation:** 10–12 days; female incubates

**Fledging:** 11–17 days; female and male feed the young

**Migration:** non-migrator to partial migrator; small flocks of up to 20 birds move around to find food

**Food:** seeds, insects; will come to seed feeders

**Compare:** Male Yellow Warbler (p. 305) is all yellow with orange streaking on chest. Pine Siskin (p. 89) has a streaked chest and belly, with yellow wing bars. The female House Finch (p. 91) and female Purple Finch (p. 111) both have heavily streaked chests.

**Stan's Notes:** A common backyard resident. Most often found in open fields, scrubby areas and woodlands. Enjoys Nyjer seed in feeders. Lines its nest with the silky down from wild thistle. Almost always in small flocks. Twitters while it flies. Flight is roller coaster-like. Often called Wild Canary due to the male's canary-colored plumage. Male sings a pleasant, high-pitched song.

# Common Yellowthroat
*Geothlypis trichas*

SUMMER

**Size:** 5" (13 cm)

**Male:** Olive-brown with a bright-yellow throat and chest, a white belly and a distinctive black mask outlined in white. Long, thin, pointed black bill.

**Female:** similar to male but lacks a black mask

**Juvenile:** same as female

**Nest:** cup; female builds; 2 broods per year

**Eggs:** 3–5; white with brown markings

**Incubation:** 11–12 days; female incubates

**Fledging:** 10–11 days; female and male feed the young

**Migration:** complete, to southern states, Mexico and Central America

**Food:** insects

**Compare:** The male American Goldfinch (p. 301) has a black forehead and wings. The Yellow-rumped Warbler (p. 213) only has patches of yellow and lacks the yellow chest of the Yellowthroat. Yellow Warbler (p. 305) has fine orange streaks on chest and lacks the black mask.

**Stan's Notes:** A common warbler of open fields and marshes. Sings a cheerful, well-known "witchity-witchity-witchity-witchity" song from deep within tall grasses. Male sings from prominent perches and while he hunts. He performs a curious courtship display, bouncing in and out of tall grass while singing a mating song. Female builds a nest low to the ground. Young remain dependent on their parents longer than most other warblers. A frequent cowbird host. Usually quiet and secretive during winter.

male

female

# Yellow Warbler
*Setophaga petechia*

SUMMER

**Size:** 5" (13 cm)

**Male:** Yellow with thin, orange streaks on the chest and belly. Long, pointed dark bill.

**Female:** same as male but lacks orange streaks

**Juvenile:** similar to female but much duller

**Nest:** cup; female builds; 1 brood per year

**Eggs:** 4–5; white with brown markings

**Incubation:** 11–12 days; female incubates

**Fledging:** 10–12 days; female and male feed the young

**Migration:** complete, to southern states, Mexico, and Central and South America

**Food:** insects

**Compare:** Yellow-rumped Warbler (p. 213) has only spots of yellow, compared with the orange streaking on the chest of male Yellow Warbler. The male American Goldfinch (p. 301) has a black forehead and black wings. The female American Goldfinch (p. 301) has white wing bars. Look for the orange streaks on the chest to identify the male Yellow Warbler.

**Stan's Notes:** Scattered but widespread warbler in Missouri. Seen in shrubby areas close to water, gardens and backyards. Zooms around shrubs and shorter trees. A prolific insect eater, gleaning caterpillars and other insects from tree leaves. Male sings loudly, flies off to grab a bug, and then starts singing again. Male sings a string of notes that sound like "sweet, sweet, sweet, I'm-so-sweet!" Begins to migrate south in August; returns in late April. Males arrive in spring before females to claim territories. Migrates at night in mixed flocks of warblers. Rests and feeds during the day.

male
p. 269

female

# American Redstart

*Setophaga ruticilla*

**Size:** 5" (13 cm)

**Female:** Olive-brown warbler with yellow patches on the sides, wings and tail. White belly.

**Male:** black with orange patches on the sides, wings and tail; white belly

**Juvenile:** same as female; male attains orange tinges in the second year

**Nest:** cup; female builds; 1 brood per year

**Eggs:** 3–5; off-white with brown markings

**Incubation:** 12 days; female incubates

**Fledging:** 9 days; female and male feed the young

**Migration:** complete, to Mexico, Central America and South America

**Food:** insects, seeds, occasionally berries

**Compare:** The female Yellow-rumped Warbler (p. 213) is similar, but it has a yellow patch on its rump. Look for yellow patches on the sides, wings and tail to help identify the female Redstart.

SUMMER

**Stan's Notes:** A common and widespread warbler in the state. Found in woodlands, parks and yards and at forest edges. Prefers large, unbroken tracts of forest. Appears hyperactive when it feeds, hovering and darting back and forth to glean insects from leaves. Often droops wings and fans tail before launching out to catch an insect. Look for the flashing black-and-orange colors of the male high up in trees. First-year males have yellow markings and look like the females. Sings a high-pitched song that builds in intensity and then suddenly ends.

# Dickcissel

*Spiza americana*

SUMMER

**Size:** 6" (15 cm)

**Male:** A small, thick-billed bird with yellow chest, belly and eyebrows. A distinctive black bib under a white chin. Chestnut wings.

**Female:** same as male, but lacking the black bib

**Juvenile:** similar to female, only duller overall

**Nest:** cup, made of plant stems, grass and leaves; female builds; 1 brood per year

**Eggs:** 4–6; pale blue without markings

**Incubation:** 12–13 days; female incubates

**Fledging:** 9–11 days; female feeds young

**Migration:** complete, to Mexico, Central America and South America

**Food:** insects, seeds

**Compare:** The Eastern Meadowlark (p. 319) is larger and has a prominent black V-shaped necklace unlike the Dickcissel's black bib.

**Stan's Notes:** Originally a bird of the prairie, now found in alfalfa fields, abandoned fields and meadows due to the loss of native prairie habitat. Prefers habitat that is sparsely vegetative. Doesn't do well in thick, dense vegetation. The males arrive at breeding sites a couple weeks before the females and begin to sing from prominent perches. Often seen singing from a fence post because it's the tallest object around. Nest is bulky, only a couple feet above ground and usually well concealed. Common name comes from an imitation of its song.

female

male
p. 279

# Scarlet Tanager
*Piranga olivacea*

SUMMER

**Size:** 7" (18 cm)

**Female:** Drab greenish yellow with olive wings and tail. Whitish wing linings. Dark eyes.

**Male:** bright scarlet with coal-black wings and tail, an ivory bill and dark eyes

**Juvenile:** same as female

**Nest:** cup; female builds; 1 brood per year

**Eggs:** 4–5; blue-green with brown markings

**Incubation:** 13–14 days; female incubates

**Fledging:** 9–11 days; female and male feed the young

**Migration:** complete, to Central and South America

**Food:** insects, fruit

**Compare:** The female Baltimore Oriole (p. 313) has gray-brown wings. The female American Goldfinch (p. 301) has white wing bars. Look for the olive wings to identify the female Tanager.

**Stan's Notes:** A tropical-looking bird found in mature deciduous woodlands, where it hunts for insects high up in trees. Requires a territory covering at least 4 acres (1.5 ha) for nesting but prefers 8 acres (3 ha). Arrives late in spring and leaves early in fall. Both the female and male sing like American Robins, but the tanagers intersperse an unusual "chick-burr" call in their songs. The song of the female is like that of the male, only softer. This bird is one of hundreds of tanager species in the world. Nearly all are brightly colored and live in the tropics. The name "Tanager" comes from a South American Tupi Indian word meaning "any small, brightly colored bird." The male sheds (molts) his bright-scarlet plumage in the fall, appearing more like the female during winter.

male
p. 271

female

# Baltimore Oriole
*Icterus galbula*

|  |  |
|---|---|
| **Size:** | 7–8" (18–20 cm) |
| **Female:** | Pale yellow with orange tones and gray-brown wings with white wing bars. Gray bill. Dark eyes. |
| **Male:** | flaming orange with a black head and back, white-and-orange wing bars, an orange-and-black tail, a gray bill and dark eyes |
| **Juvenile:** | same as female |
| **Nest:** | pendulous; female builds; 1 brood per year |
| **Eggs:** | 4–5; bluish with brown markings |
| **Incubation:** | 12–14 days; female incubates |
| **Fledging:** | 12–14 days; female and male feed the young |
| **Migration:** | complete, to Mexico, Central America and South America |
| **Food:** | insects, fruit, nectar; comes to nectar, orange-half, and grape-jelly feeders |
| **Compare:** | The female Orchard Oriole (p. 315) has a dull-yellow belly. Look for the gray-brown wings to identify the female Baltimore Oriole. |

**Stan's Notes:** A fantastic songster, often heard before seen. Easily attracted to bird feeders that offer sugar water (nectar), orange halves or grape jelly. Parents bring young to feeders. Sits at the tops of trees, feeding on caterpillars. Female builds        lik nest at the outermost branches of tall trees. Prefers p and forests and often returns to the same area year Some of the last birds to arrive in spring (March/April) a leave in fall (August).

male
p. 273

female

first-year
male

# Orchard Oriole

*Icterus spurius*

SUMMER

**Size:** 7–8" (18–20 cm)

**Female:** Olive-green with a dull-yellow belly. Gray wings with 2 indistinct white wing bars. Long, thin bill with a gray mark on the lower bill.

**Male:** dark orange with black head, throat, upper back, wings and tail; 1 white wing bar

**Juvenile:** same as female; first-year male looks like the female, with a black bib

**Nest:** pendulous; female builds; 1 brood per year

**Eggs:** 3–5; pale blue to white, brown markings

**Incubation:** 11–12 days; female and male incubate

**Fledging:** 11–14 days; female and male feed the young

**Migration:** complete, to central Mexico, Central America and northern South America

**Food:** insects, fruit, nectar; comes to nectar, orange-half, and grape-jelly feeders

**Compare:** Female Baltimore Oriole (p. 313) is similar, but it has orange tones and more-distinct wing bars. The female Summer Tanager (p. 317) is mustard-yellow with a larger bill. Female Scarlet Tanager (p. 311) has olive wings.

**Stan's Notes:** Named "Orchard" for its preference for orchards. Also likes open woods. Eats insects until wild fruit starts to ripen. One of the last birds to arrive in spring and one of the first to leave in fall. Spends 4–5 months in Missouri. Often nests alone; sometimes nests in small colonies. Parents bring their young to bird feeding stations after they fledge. Many people don't see these birds at feeders much during the summer and think they have left, but the birds are still there, hunting for insects to feed to their young.

male
p. 281

female

# Summer Tanager
*Piranga rubra*

SUMMER

**Size:** 8" (20 cm)

**Female:** Some show a faint wash of red, but most females are a mustard-yellow overall with slightly darker wings.

**Male:** bright rosy-red bird with darker red wings

**Juvenile:** male has patches of red and green over the entire body, female is same as adult female

**Nest:** cup; female builds; 1–2 broods per year

**Eggs:** 3–5; pale blue with dark markings

**Incubation:** 10–12 days; female incubates

**Fledging:** 12–15 days; female and male feed young

**Migration:** complete, to Central and South America

**Food:** insects, fruit

**Compare:** Slightly larger than female Scarlet Tanager (p. 311), which has darker wings and a drab greenish-yellow head, back and rump. Similar to female Orchard Oriole (p. 315) and Baltimore Oriole (p. 313), but female Summer Tanager lacks wing bars and has a larger, thicker bill.

**Stan's Notes:** Found throughout the summer in Missouri forests, especially in mixed hickory-oak woods. Due to clearing of land for agriculture, populations have decreased for over a century and especially most recently. Returning to the state in late April and with young hatching in late May, some pairs have two broods per year. While fruit makes up some of the diet, most of it consists of insects such as bees and wasps. More common in Missouri than Scarlet Tanagers. Summer Tanagers unfortunately seem to be parasitized by Brown-headed Cowbirds.

**YEAR-ROUND**

# Eastern Meadowlark
*Sturnella magna*

**Size:** 9" (23 cm)

**Male:** Robin-shaped bird with a brown back and yellow chest and belly. V-shaped black necklace. Short tail with white outer tail feathers, best seen when flying away.

**Female:** same as male

**Juvenile:** same as adult

**Nest:** cup, on the ground in dense cover; female builds; 2 broods per year

**Eggs:** 3–5; white with brown markings

**Incubation:** 13–15 days; female incubates

**Fledging:** 11–12 days; female and male feed the young

**Migration:** complete, to southern states, Mexico, Central America; non-migrator in Missouri

**Food:** insects, seeds

**Compare:** This is the only large yellow bird that has a black V mark on the breast.

**Stan's Notes:** A songbird of open grassy country, singing when perched and in flight. Given the name "Meadowlark" because it's a bird of meadows and sings like the larks of Europe. Best known for its wonderful, clear, flute-like whistling song. Often seen perching on fence posts but will quickly dive into tall grass when approached. Sometimes domes its nest with dried grass. Not in the lark family. A member of the blackbird family, related to grackles and orioles. The Western Meadowlark is nearly identical in appearance and sings a different song. Western Meadowlarks can be found in northwestern Missouri.

## ABOUT THE AUTHOR

Naturalist, wildlife photographer and writer Stan Tekiela is the originator of the popular state-specific field guide series that includes the *Trees of Missouri Field Guide*. Stan has authored more than 190 educational books, including field guides, quick guides, nature books, children's books, and more, presenting many species of animals and plants.

With a Bachelor of Science degree in natural history from the University of Minnesota and as an active professional naturalist for more than 30 years, Stan studies and photographs wildlife throughout the United States and Canada. He has received national and regional awards for his books and photographs and is also a well-known columnist and radio personality. His syndicated column appears in more than 25 newspapers, and his wildlife programs are broadcast on a number of Midwest radio stations. You can follow Stan on Facebook and Twitter or contact him via his website, naturesmart.com.

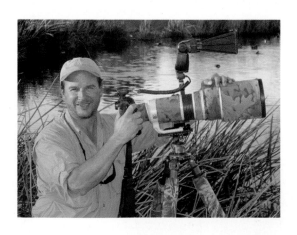